KNOW YOUR NUMBERS

Zoe Whitman

Know Your Numbers

Copyright Zoe Whitman © 2020

ISBN 978-1-912009-98-5

First Published by Compass-Publishing 2020
www.compass-publishing.com

Printed in the United Kingdom

A catalogue version of the book can be found at the British Library

Designed by The Book Refinery Ltd
www.thebookrefinery.com

For Olly, Heidi and Wilf

Tell me something. Which one word sums up how you feel when you think about bookkeeping?

FOREWORD

Procrastination is the thief of time. I know it is because at the age of about fifteen I had to write it out one thousand times as a punishment for being late handing in my homework. Some fifty years later, here I am passing on this nugget of information, this guiding principle by which to guide your life.

The truth is that most of us do the things we enjoy, because these are the things we do well, or at least better. So why waste our time procrastinating about things that don't motivate us or are spoiled by being done badly? Having run my own businesses for most of my life, I learned early on that being a jack of all trades really only means that we master none of them.

When I had my first car, my father spent hours showing me how to change the oil or the brake pads but very soon I realised that I had more time to drive the car if I paid someone else to do the maintenance for me. Okay, so it cost me money, but as a result I had much more fun in the car and I knew that whoever carried out the work was trained, knew the best methods for doing the work, and took half the time I did to do it. Bookkeeping is no different.

The first time I really met Zoe was when she came onto stage at our annual conference to be presented by me with the LUCA Award for Small Practice of the Year. We had recognised her as a rising star. We then invited Zoe to join one of our ICB technical panels, so that we could use her insight and experience. She had not long given birth but, undaunted by this and keen to share her knowledge with others, she joined the meeting by video. Entering the meeting about half way through, I was amused to see Zoe on the tv screen, complete with sleeping baby on her shoulder. That sums up Zoe and it sums up bookkeepers; unfazed, ordered and eager to help.

Zoe is a doer and has written a great book; *Know Your Numbers* is an explanation of what you need to do to give your business the best possible chance of surviving in your hands. If you're inspired by Zoe's words and explanations, great. Have fun with your books. But if not, don't worry. There are more than five million businesses in the UK and around 95% of them are microbusinesses. Most are run by single individuals who don't have time to do everything themselves.

The bookkeeping profession is changing almost daily and the likelihood that you can keep ahead of the changes in legislation, best practice and digitalisation, whilst at the same time giving 110% to your business, is disappearing fast. Find a good bookkeeper that you like and trust and leave it to them. You have enough to do.

But first, read this book. At least then you can make a considered choice as to whether you want to master everything, or just everything but the books.

GARRY CARTER

Co-Founder and President

The Institute of Certified Bookkeepers

CONTENTS

INTRODUCTION

The world is divided into two groups of people. When faced with the Sunday newspaper, there are those who search out the Sudoku puzzle and those who would rather do the crossword.

Having worked as an accountant for almost half my life, I know how problematic numbers can be for those who are not mathematically minded. Anything numbers-related, even for experts at the top of their profession who are totally academic in every other way, can induce a sense of fear and panic.

Finance, business's equivalent of maths, has an air of secrecy around it; people who know about business finance seem to be in an elite club. If you don't understand it, finance can seem complicated and overwhelming, as though ruled by hidden codes, impenetrable unless you have an accountancy degree.

Let me tell you something, though. Accountancy and bookkeeping have, more often than not, absolutely nothing to do with maths (except for a very small amount of addition and subtraction). You don't need to be a mathematical genius to do my job. What you do need is a clear knowledge of the necessary rules and how to apply them. If you can do that, you can cover the basics with few difficulties. Finance has a bad reputation and if you've been led to believe you'll never be able to understand it, you're not alone.

I've held senior accountancy positions in large organisations. Now I run a bookkeeping practice called '*But the Books*',[1] where I apply big business principles to small businesses without making it complicated. I keep finance simple because I truly believe that finance can be simple.

Business owners need to know their numbers. They need to know how much they're selling, how profitable they are, and how much spare money is

---

1. But the Books - www.butthebooks.co.uk

in the bank. Because if you don't know whether you're about to run out of cash in two months' time, how can you possibly make decisions about your business's future?

I've worked with over 50 small businesses since starting out in 2017, helping them not only with their accounts, tax returns, budgets and forecasts, but also to really understand what's going on in their businesses. Through this work I've really learnt which things business owners prioritise, which worries keep them up at night, and which struggles they face day to day. I felt like all of this experience should be brought together in one place so that I can share my knowledge with more and more small business owners. So, here it is!

A little while ago I set up an accounting system for a client who, up until that point, had been using a spreadsheet which she updated once at the end of every financial year. Although she had a sense of her monthly income, she didn't really know what her costs were or how much profit she was making. This client, let's call her Sarah, ran a shop and during our meetings it transpired that she had no stock control process, meaning that she had little idea of what her items costed or for how long she'd had them. When I suggested that she should be doing a stock-take every quarter in order that she could understand her costs and profit figures, Sarah broke down in tears. Up until that point, she'd coped really well with setting up the accounting system. But, the task of stock-taking—probably the one task which had been on her mind all along—was the tipping point and the thing which brought her the most anxiety.

For me, a stock-take is a routine, mandatory task where there's no emotion; I count items and work out how much stock a business is holding. But when you haven't done a stock-take for years or don't know how to do a stock-take, it can be overwhelming. If perhaps you feel ashamed because you know it's a thing you should have been doing but haven't, it can really be quite an emotional affair.

Sarah's story is one of the many reasons why I've written this book. I want to remove the emotion around finance and ensure that you have the right information so that you not only comply with the rules but also understand your business more clearly. I want you to have a system you can follow every month so that you feel less overwhelmed and more in control. And it would make my day if I could take it one step further and help you start to use those numbers to understand your business more, set some targets and really succeed in what you do.

Why you should read this book

In this book I'm going to help you with the bookkeeping for your small business. I'm going to show you how to set up an accounting system, how to deal with your bag of receipts and, most importantly, help you understand and feel in control of your business's finances so that you can make decisions about the future.

When I was researching for this book, I found plenty of material on bookkeeping for small businesses. However, I found it to be either inaccessible and loaded with jargon or several hundred pages of very dry step-by-step tutorials. This book is different because I'm not going to try to teach you how to be a bookkeeper. My aim is to make sure that you feel more comfortable about what you need to be doing from week to week (and month to month) without getting too technical.

As we go through, I'm going to share client stories—I've changed clients' names and sometimes the details of their businesses—to show you that you're not alone in the issues you're facing and the questions you have, and also to demonstrate how our customers have benefited from improving their bookkeeping processes.

In Chapter 1 we're going to look at what you want to achieve, what you want to get out of reading this book and how you want your processes around bookkeeping to improve. I'm going to share lots of client stories in this section because I think there's so much that can be learned from different people we've worked with.

When I started writing this book, I asked our Instagram followers to tell me one word which summed up how they felt when they thought of bookkeeping. They said things like 'scary', 'taxing', 'shudder', 'fiddly' and simply 'urghhh'.

From my experience with But the Books, I know that a lot of people avoid their bookkeeping, they're intimidated by their figures, and they experience a mental block when faced with a page of numbers. In Chapter 2 we're going to talk about how to approach your numbers logically and without emotion so that you can get into good bookkeeping habits and no longer feel afraid of looking at your books.

You probably had a number of questions when starting up your business; Chapter 3 will give you some answers. I'm frequently asked about which legal structure to choose, how different types of businesses are taxed and how to pay yourself from each. This chapter will set out the differences between working as a sole trader versus working through a limited company so that you can make an informed decision about the best structure for you.

In Chapter 4 we'll consider whether you should be using accounting software. Most businesses start off with a spreadsheet, and in fact many bookkeepers and accounting firms provide their clients with spreadsheets to keep track of their business finances. In Chapter 4 we'll look at the pros and cons of spreadsheets, why an accounting system might be better, what to look for when choosing one and whether it's worth paying for software.

One of our clients' biggest struggles is dealing with paperwork and receipts. I can't tell you how many people have come to me with a carrier bag or a shoebox (or several), and the state of their accounting records is causing them stress or making them feel overwhelmed. Chapter 5 will help you overcome your worries as we look at how to deal with your bag of receipts for good.

I can't help you get on top of your bookkeeping without telling you a bit about accountancy so in Chapter 6 we'll get a bit (but not too) technical and I'll talk through some of the important things you need to know about bookkeeping. We'll look at the main accounting reports—the Profit and Loss report and the Balance Sheet—and I'll talk you through some common mistakes so that you don't make them.

Chapter 7 is a walk through the bookkeeping tasks you need to do for your business each week or month to stay on top of things. I cover each of the key areas—invoicing, purchases and banking— so that, by the end, you have a simple bookkeeping process to follow.

Bookkeeping isn't just about recording transactions; having good records means that you can use your figures to tell you things about your business. In Chapter 8 we'll look at which reports you can run, including your Profit and Loss report and Balance Sheet, and how to understand and interpret the numbers they contain to give a bigger, better picture of your business.

Once you understand your accounts, you might like to start thinking about some goals for the business's profits. Our clients often ask questions about the future, like how their bank balance will look in three months' time or how it will change if they take one course of action or another. Chapter 9 covers how to set a budget and a cash flow forecast so that you feel able to plan ahead.

Chapter 10 takes this even further by helping you set specific key performance indicators. These are targets for your business which you can monitor and measure to learn more about your business and compare its performance against different time periods, against your goals and against other businesses. There are all sorts of things you can track but we'll talk about deciding which KPIs are most important for your business. That way, you can have a realistic, manageable number of KPIs to track from month to month.

Bookkeeping isn't for everyone, and you may well get to a point where you decide that actually you don't have the time or expertise to do it yourself and thus choose to outsource. With this in mind, Chapter 11 talks about how to find a great bookkeeper for your business, what a bookkeeper can do for you, and how to make the most out of your relationship with your bookkeeper, starting with that very first meeting.

Whatever your circumstances, I want you to get to the end of this book feeling a sense of relief, with a plan for what to do next, whether this means tackling that bag of receipts, setting up an accounting system, or organising an initial chat with a great bookkeeper.

Who's this book for?

If you're a sole trader, a partner in a partnership, or an owner of a small limited company turning over up to £1m or so per year, this book is for you. The principles of bookkeeping are the same across different legal business forms, although the way you account for things (or record them) can vary depending on your circumstances. Although this book will not give you tax advice, I will highlight where there are important differences so that you can seek professional advice to help you with your specific needs.

Remember: bookkeeping is not maths. Sure, there's a bit of adding up involved, but if you're not keen on trigonometry, it isn't going to be a problem. So, fear not and let's get started.

CHAPTER 1
WHAT DO YOU WANT TO ACHIEVE?

You picked up this book because you want to get your finances organised. Maybe the way you scrambled to complete last year's tax return is a process you never want to repeat. Perhaps you have piles of paper everywhere and no real system in place. Or, it could be that you prioritise anything and everything over invoicing and, all too often, find that there's no money in the bank account and one of your clients hasn't paid you for three months. All of these are reasons why business owners come to me at But the Books.

This book will help you with all of these issues and I urge you to keep the vision of your organised set of finances in mind as you read. It'll keep you focussed on reading every page and it will help you to devise a course of action to achieve your goal.

In this chapter I'll talk about how to get on top of your bookkeeping: what to do, when to do it and whether you're the right person for each task. By the end of this chapter, you'll know exactly which steps to take in order to organise your finances and I hope that you'll feel empowered and motivated to make the necessary changes.

What's your motivation?

All businesses must keep accounting records. At the very least, you need to be able to prepare your tax return (if you're a sole trader) or your company accounts and corporation tax return (if you run a limited company). When I run our workshop, 'Bookkeeping for Startups', I always start by asking people why they come along. Everyone in the room has an awareness that they need to be doing something, that they're not doing things right, or that they don't know what they need to be doing.

But, when I dig further, I often find that it's more than just the fact that they saw the workshop was running and thought it would be a good idea to come along. They tell me that they're overwhelmed and that they haven't done any bookkeeping since they started their business. Someone even once told me she was afraid she'd go to jail because she hadn't kept her records up to date. I'm sure she was joking but behind that joke was a real fear about numbers, bookkeeping and taxes and she felt out of her depth.

You picked up this book for a reason and it's important to remember what that reason was. Keeping that reason at the front of your mind will keep you focussed as you read the next chapters of this book and will see you through the process.

Client story – Megan

Megan teaches individuals to play the guitar. As well as teaching traditional music lessons to children in schools, she holds independent lessons with adults from her home and she performs with a band. She also arranges workshops and sometimes hires another music teacher to run them on her behalf. As a sole trader, her main concern was being able to draw a monthly wage from her business. When she came to us, Megan knew that she had money in the bank but she didn't know how much profit she was making per month. She also wanted to know which of her different teaching methods were most profitable and whether hiring somebody to run her workshops was worthwhile.

Client story – Andy

Andy is a freelance designer and when we first met he was struggling to stay on top of his cash flow. He was raising invoices on time but as clients were given 30 days to pay and were often paying him late, he was finding it very difficult to predict how much money would be coming into his bank account and when. He'd also signed up to various subscriptions but had lost track of which payments would be taken from his bank account and on which date. Andy is VAT registered, so also needed to pay his quarterly VAT bill and, on occasion, he found that he didn't have the necessary money in the bank.

Client story – Jen

Invoicing was the source of problems for our client, Jen. Most months, she raised up to twenty invoices for jobs ranging from £100 to a few thousand. As many of the invoices were for the same amount (£100 or £200), it was difficult for her to identify which clients had actually paid her and after a few months of not keeping up-to-date records, her outstanding invoices had become overwhelming. When we met Jen, she didn't know who to chase up for payment and she was almost afraid to do so in case the client had actually paid, resulting in embarrassment for her and potential damage to their working relationship and any opportunity for future work.

The reasons why people decide to take control of their bookkeeping are varied, but one of these client stories might resonate with you. Whether it's to do with understanding your profit margins, or staying on top of your cash flow or invoicing, knowing the problem areas in your business will help to bring a focus to your bookkeeping efforts.

Once you've got a bookkeeping process in place, we can take things one step further because there's so much more that efficient bookkeeping will allow you to do. In Chapters 8-10, we'll look at how you can use your records to understand your business and to analyse profit, sales, costs and cash flow. All of these things will make setting up your bookkeeping process more worthwhile and will give you even more reason to remain motivated to stay on top of your bookkeeping in the future.

When will you do your bookkeeping?

Bookkeeping is one of those business admin tasks which is hard to prioritise over what you, as a business owner, see as the 'real work': running your business. It's difficult to put bookkeeping before completing a job for a client or pursuing a new client lead and that's why small business owners often come to us and say they haven't done any bookkeeping for six months.

However, not doing your bookkeeping means that you have no insight into how your business is doing, i.e. what's working and what's not. It means you won't know how profitable you are, whether you're getting enough work to cover your costs, whether you'll have the money to pay salaries next month or whether you're about to have a major cash flow crisis.

Have you ever decided to take a new fitness class and failed to stick to it? The intention was there but in practice the motivation was lacking? I've been there. In 2010, I ran the London Marathon, which was a huge physical and mental challenge for me as I'd only run a half marathon previously. The only way to build up to that distance was to schedule some serious training. I joined a running club for two shorter evening runs, and committed to a longer run every Saturday morning. My fellow runners held me accountable, challenging me if I didn't turn up, and I told everyone about my Saturday morning runs because the more I said it, the more I believed it would happen. It would have been very easy for me to make excuses to avoid a 20-mile run and have a lie-in, but in reality I wanted it to happen because running the London Marathon felt like an important thing for me to achieve.

Because we know how easy it is to make excuses and prioritise other things, at But the Books we recommend that our clients set time aside for their accounts every week. Just like I did when I trained for the marathon, I recommend that you book a non-negotiable appointment in your diary. I believe it's the only way to form a new habit successfully. It might help even more if you ask somebody to be present at said appointment or to serve as your accountability partner, checking in with you to ensure that you stick to the plan.

I'm often asked how much time is needed to do bookkeeping every week. The answer: it depends on the number of transactions you need to process and the complexity of your business. You might need an hour or you might need a whole afternoon – it's going to be trial and error at first. If you overestimate, you can use the remaining time to indulge yourself with something you love to do as a reward for sticking to your appointment. Staying on top of things weekly is critical if you're going to have a thorough understanding of your business.

I promise you, if you don't dedicate time in your diary for this (or get someone else to), you will find something 'better' to do, so the question is: when will be the best time for you to do your bookkeeping each week?

In order to decide, ask yourself:

» *Do I work best in the mornings or afternoons?*

» *Which other commitments do I have to work around?*

» *Am I in a better frame of mind for this kind of task first thing on a Monday or will this conflict with a time I like to be doing something else, such as planning for the week?*

» *Is it realistic to think I'll do my bookkeeping last thing on a Friday or am I more likely to want to do something else, like head off for a drink with the team?*

Personally, I schedule our bookkeeping for last thing on a Thursday. I don't work on Fridays at the moment and I find the end of the week is a good time to reflect on what's happened, to raise invoices and to finish off any outstanding tasks. I'd rather do it at the end of the day than just after lunch because I find it difficult to sit down and focus just after a meal and prefer instead to be talking to people around that time.

Being realistic about the time of week and time of day you're able to concentrate most is crucial to scheduling a time which you'll stick to. I'd really suggest having a think about when you're best suited to tasks like this because if you are focussed and your head's in a good place, it will take you less time than when you're tired, easily distracted or don't want to be sitting in front of the computer screen.

Who's best to do your bookkeeping?

Most small business owners take on the bookkeeping themselves (or enlist their spouse or another family member) when they start out and it's likely that you have done the same, too. Money is often tight for start-ups, so it makes sense that you would try to do things yourself or ask favours from family members, particularly if you know somebody who is good with numbers. However, it's important to question whether this person is the right person for the job.

Client story – Eddie

Eddie's a retailer and his wife used to do his books, but when things got complicated, she didn't want to do the bookkeeping anymore and neither did Eddie. By the time we were called in to help, Eddie had a four-month backlog of transactions to deal with and an overdue VAT return. We were able to get Eddie's accounts up to date in a relatively short amount of time but by that time Eddie's VAT return was late.

When you're deciding who will do your bookkeeping, ask yourself:

» *Do you/they want to do the bookkeeping?*

» *Do they have the time to do it well?*

» *Will they want to keep doing the bookkeeping once the novelty's worn off or when there's an impending deadline when they'd rather be doing something else?*

» *Are you confident that they have the skills and expertise to do the bookkeeping properly?*

It's critical that you can answer yes to all of these questions, otherwise you should rethink who you're going to appoint as your bookkeeper.

If you can understand your motivations for setting up a bookkeeping system, and you can find the right person to do that bookkeeping at a time they're likely to be most committed and productive, you have the best possible chance of success.

Summary

In this chapter we've looked at why you need to set up a bookkeeping process, whether you're the right person to do your bookkeeping going forward and how you will remain focussed on keeping your bookkeeping process up to date in the future. In the next chapter we'll remain focussed on the subject of motivation and look at why some people struggle with money and numbers. After that, we'll move on to look at which records you need to keep and how to set up a bookkeeping process.

CHAPTER 2
WHY DO PEOPLE STRUGGLE WITH MONEY AND NUMBERS?

I can't tell you how many people find money, finance and bookkeeping overwhelming. If you read the reviews on our 'But The Books' Google or Facebook pages, you will see people describing how finance leaves them flummoxed, that they tend to bury their heads in the sand when it comes to the numbers, that they're not technically minded, that they don't feel confident, that they don't know where to start and that the finance side of running a business can even make them feel sick. Do any of these sound like you?

In this chapter we're going to look at why finance is a subject people do not always think about logically and rationally and we'll talk about how to start to remove the emotion from dealing with your business's finances.

Obviously, finance isn't something that I struggle with, but I can tell you honestly that I do know how you feel. The thing that I find complicated in business is the legal side of things. When I had to review our terms and conditions recently, I can't tell you how much I dragged my feet. Even once I'd spoken to the solicitor and I knew exactly what I needed to do—there were only three or four things to change—I procrastinated, and when I did finally send out our revised terms and conditions, I realised that this job had been on my to-do list for four months.

So, if you've been procrastinating about getting the bookkeeping for your business sorted, you're not alone. We've had clients who've failed to turn up at meetings because they've been afraid to talk about the reality of their finances. We have clients who have been in business for over a year and had never done any bookkeeping until they engaged with us. Several of our clients have become tearful in meetings, not because we told them bad news, but because the idea of starting a new process takes them completely out of their comfort zone. One of our clients told me that she felt like she was bringing her dirty laundry when she started working with us. Truthfully, I can say that nothing phases me anymore; no matter how bad your accounting records are, we've seen it all before and we're here to help.

People don't just feel like this about their business's finances. They feel like this about their personal finances too, particularly if things aren't going well. At school, finance isn't prioritised; we don't learn about how to manage household or business finances. Plenty of people don't budget in their personal lives, surviving from month to month and assuming that things must be going okay if there's money in the bank account. It's the same for many business owners. If you're okay with surviving from month to month and you're able to do what you need to do for your business, then that's fine, you don't need to read anymore.

But are you lying awake at night, worrying about whether you'll be able to pay yourself this month? Do you worry whether you'll be able to pay your tax bill, your suppliers or your staff? Do you feel sick at the thought of doing a tax return? Have you never done a stock-take in your shop? Were you late submitting your tax return last year because you had to spend every evening for three weeks doing your accounts for the whole year before you could file it? Are you unsure what to include on an invoice, or if your customers aren't paying you? If the answer to any of these questions is yes, then read on because I can help.

The emotions behind money

Finance is a subject we expect to think about rationally; after all, put simply, finance is about 'money in' and 'money out'. But, in reality, for most people money is an emotional subject. If you know anything about motivation theory or if you've heard of Maslow's Hierarchy of Needs, you'll know that the most basic essentials are food and shelter, things that money *can* buy. If you don't have money, you can't provide for your most basic requirements, so it's no wonder that money stirs our emotions.

Many of us have different levels of anxiety about money in our personal lives; some people drastically overspend and some are so frugal that they won't spend the bare minimum on themselves. In some households one partner takes control of all of the money, leaving the other unable to deal with money because they've simply never had to do it, or powerless to control how their money is spent. Some people have money-related emotional baggage because money in their childhood was lacking, or they had too much... need I go on? In short, it's complicated and it's emotional, and this makes it difficult for us to be rational about money and finance in our private lives and also in business.

One of the ways in which we, as humans, regulate our emotions is to avoid information and situations which make us feel negative. If you have negative feelings about money, whatever they may be, you're more likely to want to avoid taking control of your finances. This leads to more anxiety and more bad feeling and, ultimately, this can result in an endless cycle of helplessness and financial chaos.

What if you can't move forwards?

In this book I'm going to help you take a rational and logical approach to organising your finances. We're simply going to talk about what you need to do and how to do it, and I'm going to tell you some stories about our clients to help you realise that you are not alone. Along the way, I'll offer you some steps that you can follow, but I suggest that you stand back and look at your business's finances as if you're a completely unrelated third party. Imagine that you're being paid to do the job for somebody else. Make it a job with a deadline and view each transaction and each piece of paper as what they are in their simplest form: some 'money in' or some 'money out' of the business.

We know, from working with many clients who have a backlog of transactions to record, that the idea of ploughing through that paperwork can feel daunting and overwhelming. You might also be worried about what you'll find out about your business's finances when you get to the end of the process. We have found that this is a big reason why people procrastinate about getting it sorted. But, in my experience, business owners feel so much better once they have cleared that backlog, have a system in place, and understand what their numbers show them about their business. This gives them back control. Even if they discover something negative—the business has cash flow problems or it isn't profitable or it is simply spending too much—they are in a place where they can make a plan and take action. And we find that, generally, business owners don't want to return to their old ways and they do their best to stay motivated to keep on top of their bookkeeping.

Client story – Gemma and Andrea

Gemma and her sister, Andrea, run a reclaimed furniture store. When I first met them, they told me that they hadn't been keeping their bookkeeping up to date and had just had a terrible time preparing their year-end accounts. They were determined to avoid a last-minute dash again, so asked us to set up an accounting system for them, which duly we did over the next couple of weeks.

At one of our meetings, we discussed the stock held in the shop, and I asked where we would find details of their costs so that we could record them accurately in the new system. Gemma and Andrea had built up their stock over the course of two years, sometimes buying job lots at auction or markets. Gemma had memorised the prices they'd paid, and had never written them down anywhere or devised a system to record this information. We established that somebody would need to complete a stock-take and this was something Gemma found quite overwhelming. For somebody who was convinced she didn't have a head for numbers, it was an emotional subject.

Gemma and Andrea decided that one of their part-time employees should be tasked with stock-taking. As somebody who wasn't invested in the shop financially or emotionally, the employee was able to put together a record of all of the shop's stock. Then, it was fairly straightforward for Gemma to run through the list and assign costs to the different items without it being a daunting task.

Identifying that stock taking took the business owners outside of their comfort zones and making a simple plan to delegate it to a member of staff removed the emotion from the situation. If you feel too emotionally involved in a process, it can make sense to make it into a simple step by step process that either you follow or which you can find somebody else to manage, allowing you to get what you need doing done in the business.

Summary

In this chapter we've looked at how dealing with finance, both in your business and in your personal life, can be difficult and how emotions can become tied up with anything money-related. Hopefully, you now have a better understanding of why finance can sometimes feel illogical and you feel ready to tackle your bookkeeping in a systematic, emotion-free way.

CHAPTER 3
WHAT TO THINK ABOUT WHEN
YOU START YOUR BUSINESS

For the purposes of this chapter, I'm going to assume that you haven't started your business yet or you've only just started up. Inevitably, anyone taking their first steps on their business journey will have questions about how to set things up. But, in reality, the questions I'm going to cover in this chapter are raised frequently by established businesses, too. Predominantly, this is because they made certain decisions when setting up their business— perhaps acting on the advice of a relative or trusted friend—and only later have they questioned the precise impact of those decisions.

We're going to look at the legal structure of your business and the subsequent differences regarding tax, reporting requirements and how you pay yourself. We'll also look at why a separate bank account for your business is important, if not essential.

It's incredibly exciting when you start a business. I know, I've been there. You have this idea in your mind of the thing you want to do: what you want to sell and the problem you want to solve for people. You'll be thinking about how you'll source customers, what to call your business, which platform to use to build your website, what your branding should look like, who should host your email, what you should be posting on social media, even perhaps thinking ahead to your terms and conditions. But, apart from visualising how much money you'll make, I suspect you didn't start your business because you wanted to think about the finance side of running a business.

In fact, finance is probably this dull headache you get every now and again and you plan to do something properly when your number of transactions increases. Because, at the moment, the financial year end is months away —you might not even have to submit a tax return for over a year—so it just doesn't feel worth worrying about.

As you might expect, I'm going to tell you otherwise. There are certain things which are essential to get right from day one; there are others which, sure, you can leave for a while. But if you do, you might find yourself having a mad panic to sort out your finances in time for a tax deadline just as you're entering your busiest month ever. So, let's talk about the basics so that you've given them some consideration and then you know which vital actions you should be taking right now.

Choosing a legal structure

One of the top questions I get asked is 'should I trade as a sole trader or should I set up a limited company?'. Your business's legal structure is certainly something to think about at the beginning, as it affects all sorts of things, from the way the business profits are taxed to how you can take money out.

Choosing a legal structure is a decision you should make based on the specific circumstances of your business. In this section, I'll set out the main differences between the different structures, but if you have any questions about the implications of choosing a particular legal structure for you and your business, you should speak to an accountant or solicitor.

Working as a sole trader

When people talk about being self-employed, they usually mean that they are a sole trader. When you decide to work as a sole trader, you need to register as self-employed with HMRC so that they know you're in business and can tax you appropriately.

When you're a sole trader, you and your business are legally the same entity. If your business is unable to pay its debts, creditors can recover payment for those debts from your own personal assets.

This means that business profits are your profits (or income). The money in the business bank account is your money and you can dip into it when you need to. Taking money out of the business isn't a 'wage', though, so it's not an expense of the business for the purposes of calculating business profits. It is simply taking out what we call 'drawings'. Business profits are added to your other income for the tax year and taxed through a self-assessment tax return, meaning that you pay income tax and National Insurance contributions on them. A tax year runs from April 6th until April 5th the following year.

Working in a partnership

I will touch on partnerships briefly as we do often come across businesses run as partnerships. A partnership is simply two or more self-employed people working together to run a business. It is also possible to set up a limited liability partnership which is more like a company, although we see this less frequently so won't go into detail here. When you start a partnership, you need to notify HMRC so that they can issue the partnership with a partnership number. At the end of the financial year, the partnership needs to prepare partnership accounts and submit a partnership return to HMRC and then each partner in the business will declare their share of the business profits in their own self-assessment tax return so that they can be taxed.

When you run a partnership, just like a sole trader you and your business are legally the same entity. If the business were unable to pay its debts, creditors can recover payment for those debts from either partner.

Limited companies

Limited companies need to be registered with Companies House. There are quite strict requirements for setting up a company. You can read about this in more detail on HMRC's website, (see page 42) but, in short, you'll need to consider what your company will be called, where it will be registered, who the directors will be, and how much share capital the company will issue. To form the company, you'll also need to submit a 'memorandum of association', a legal agreement of all founding shareholders, and 'articles of association', which set out the business's purpose and how the business will be run.

You and your limited company are separate legal entities. As a separate entity, the limited company can enter into contracts in its own name, but you, as a director, are directly responsible for making sure that the business is run properly.

A company's financial year is determined by when the company was originally registered, although this can be changed. Companies need to file annual accounts with Companies House at the year end and you may need an accountant to help you with this. In terms of tax, companies don't pay income tax; instead, profits are subject to corporation tax, which is calculated after the end of each financial year.

As the business's money belongs to the business and not to you, the business needs to have its own bank account and you cannot dip into these funds. The company can pay you either a salary through payroll or dividends or a combination of the two. As an individual, if you're a director of a limited company, you will need to submit a self-assessment tax return to HMRC at the end of the tax year.

There are significant differences between the available legal structures, and you need to be aware of what your choice means for you as a business owner. In our experience, many small business owners start out as sole traders, choosing to incorporate their business (a fancy way of saying set up a limited company) once they're making significant profits. The tax regimes and the reporting requirements are different for companies and sole traders and, depending on your circumstances, there will be benefits to choosing one structure over another. You should weigh up the pros and cons of each option for you.

Client story – Tom

Let me tell you about Tom. He's a sole trader and he takes commissions for artwork and sells prints online, receiving payment for them through PayPal. Tom doesn't have a separate business bank account, which is fine because this is not a requisite for sole traders. The thing is, his customers pay him into his personal current account, his PayPal account is linked to his joint account with his partner and he buys art supplies (which he gets from places like Wilko, the Range and Hobbycraft) from a combination of both accounts.

As you might expect, all of these transactions going through different bank accounts makes it difficult for Tom to keep abreast of how his business is doing from day to day. This is complicated further by the fact that Tom needs to keep careful track of which purchases are business-related and which are personal expenses. I'm sure you can see that if Tom lost a receipt for a transaction at Wilko, it could be very difficult a few weeks down the line to remember whether that transaction related to an item bought for his business or for his home.

When Tom came to us, he hadn't done any bookkeeping for the year and needed to complete his tax return. This meant going through his two bank statements to identify which transactions were and weren't business-related. We were able to do it, but the process would have been far more straightforward if Tom had dedicated a separate bank account to his business.

Opening a separate bank account

If you're going to make the process of recording your business transactions as pain-free as possible, the most straightforward way to identify those transactions is to channel them all through one separate bank account.

▶ Running a limited company?

If you're running a limited company, you do need to have a business bank account registered under the business's name. This is because the business is a separate legal entity and the business's money belongs to the business, not to you. In fact, if you're running a limited company which doesn't have a business bank account, stop reading and set up a bank account now!

▶ Sole trader?

If you're a sole trader like Tom, you could put all of your business transactions through your own personal bank account. However, it will make your life easier to use a business bank account or a separate personal bank account and avoid using it for any income or expenditure other than that related to your business.

✓ A business bank account means that you can set apart business transactions

When recording your business expenses, the last thing you want to do is to trawl through every transaction on your bank statement and try to remember whether they were for your business or not. Keeping your business transactions separate from personal ones keeps things simple.

✓ If you have a separate business bank account, you can use it to keep money aside for your tax bill

If your business is profitable, you will most likely have a tax bill to settle up at the end of the financial year. If you keep your business money separate from your personal money, it's easier to keep money aside to pay your tax bill when it's due. You don't want to get to January 31st and realise you can't pay your tax bill because you spent the money on Christmas presents! You might even consider having a second business bank account to keep some of the business's money aside just for this type of thing.

✓ A separate business bank account allows you to keep things consistent for your customers

You want to make it as simple as possible for your customers to pay you. If you set up a separate bank account for your business now and make sure that its details are the ones on your invoices, you won't have to go through the pain of informing all your customers of your new bank details down the line.

✓ A separate business bank account makes it easier to see your cash flow

If your business's money is separate from your personal money, it's much easier to see how the business is doing. At a glance you can see how much money is in the business bank account and know whether you're getting close to that overdraft.

✓ Having a separate business bank account makes budgeting easier in your personal life

A lot of business owners are also employed, particularly when they're just starting out. If you have a salary, personal bills and then business income and expenditure all going through the same account, it's much harder to keep sight of how healthy your personal bank balance is looking. If you keep your personal financial affairs separate from those of the business, and pay yourself a set monthly amount from the business (via drawings if you're a sole trader), you'll have a much better idea of what's going in and out of your personal account each month.

✓ Having a separate business bank account just makes good business sense

Keeping transactions separate keeps things cleaner, helps you budget and forecast, and improves your understanding of your business. If you ever decide to bring in a business partner or turn the business into a limited company, the business's money will be held separately and all transactions will be together in one place.

Paying yourself from your business

The way in which you pay yourself from your business depends on which kind of business structure you have in place. If you're a sole trader, you'll pay yourself through drawings and if you run a limited company, you'll pay yourself through a combination of salary and dividends.

Drawings

As previously stated, if you're a sole trader, you and your business are the same. Even if your business has separate bank accounts, the money they contain is your money. This means that you can take money out of the business bank account as and when you wish (provided, of course, that there is money to withdraw) – this is what we call 'drawings'. Drawings are not an expense of the business; small business owners often make the mistake of recording payments to themselves as a business expense, thus reducing their profits, but drawings do not affect your profit. Drawings are simply you (the business owner) taking your profits (your own money) out of the business.

When you're declaring your income from your business to HMRC, you are telling them how much profit the business made during the financial year. That profit is your income and that is the amount you will be taxed on.

Salary

If you run a limited company, you and the business are separate legal entities. This means that you can't simply take money out of the business bank accounts; instead, you need to pay yourself through payroll and/or dividends.

Payroll can be run weekly or monthly and you should ensure that it is run by somebody who understands the complexities of payroll rules and regulations. Ultimately, being on a payroll will be just like being paid by an employer. You will receive a salary or an hourly rate, depending on what your employment contract says you'll receive, and a payslip every payday, and money can be paid into your bank account on that payday. You'll be taxed through PAYE and you'll receive a P60 at the end of the year.

From the business's point of view, depending on how much you are paying yourself as a salary, the business will incur employers' National Insurance contributions, which are an additional cost to the business. The business might also be obliged to pay you a pension, which is, of course, another additional cost.

Dividends

The other option open to owners of limited companies is to receive a dividend. A dividend is a payment to shareholders out of the business's annual profit after paying corporation tax. Dividends need to be declared at a board meeting and are paid at a fixed amount per share. This means that if there are other shareholders in the business, they will receive an equivalent dividend based on the number of shares they hold.

What happens in practice is that business owners withdraw a small amount each month or quarter based on an estimate of the business's annual profits, this is known as an interim dividend. A final dividend is then declared and paid after the company's year end. Dividends are paid without any deduction of tax so they need to be declared in your self-assessment tax return. The tax rates for dividends are different than for other types of income, and your accountant or tax advisor will be able to guide you as to what is an effective combination of salary and dividends to take from your company.

Beware: if you take more money out of your business than you are able to declare as a dividend, perhaps because you overestimated how much profit the business was making, you could become liable to a tax charge on the outstanding director's loan at the end of the year, so it pays to be prudent in this area.

Summary

In this chapter we've looked at the basic considerations for when you start your business: opening a separate business bank account, the legal structure your business might take and the ways in which you can pay yourself.

In my experience, people often have a lot of questions about choosing a legal structure for their business. If you need more help, you should speak to your bookkeeper or accountant and if you need help with setting up a limited company, speak to a solicitor. HMRC also have some really useful guides to help you record the right things when you're starting out, whether you're a sole trader[2] or running a limited company[3].

---

2. HMRC's guide to setting up as a sole trader - www.gov.uk/set-up-sole-trader

3. HMRC's guide to setting up a limited company - www.gov.uk/set-up-limited-company

CHAPTER 4
SETTING UP AN ACCOUNTING SYSTEM

In my experience, there are three ways in which small business owners organise their accounting records.

Alan raises invoices in Microsoft Word and keeps his expense receipts in a carrier bag. He also has some supplier invoices in paper copy and others attached to emails which he may or may not be able to quickly access.

Becky keeps a list of income and expenditure in a spreadsheet. She creates her invoices in InDesign and emails them to her clients. She organises her receipts and invoices by saving digital copies in one place, on Google Drive, and cross-referencing them with the spreadsheet.

Charlie keeps his accounting records in an accounting system called Xero. He does some of his bookkeeping himself and has support from an accountant at the year end.

Does one of these sound like you?

More often than not, the new businesses we meet record their income and expenditure in a spreadsheet, with their paperwork in various states of filing; some business owners file alphabetically or by date, whereas others throw everything into a carrier bag or a box. We always start a conversation about whether or not they should make the move to accounting software. In this chapter I'll tell you why we favour accounting software over spreadsheets as well as discussing the benefits of the latter, whether you should pay for accounting software, which software we recommend for small businesses and how the future is digital and why you need to be prepared.

Accounting software: some of the main features

At But the Books we've worked with many clients to set them up with accounting software. When small business owners come to us, they have a range of different accounting systems and processes in place; some are pretty savvy with accounting software and others are still heavily paper-based or use old systems. Once you have a system in place, whatever that means for you, you're likely to stick with it for a long time. Change can be a chore, learning a new system takes time and getting into new habits takes discipline, but there are some really good reasons to go digital and set up accounting software.

Before we consider which software might be right for you, let's look at some of the features of accounting software which could revolutionise things for you. This way, you'll know what you should be looking for when faced with the options.

▶ **Bank feed**

You can connect your bank account to most accounting software which means that your transactions are pulled in directly from your bank statement. It's the perfect way to ensure that you don't forget to record any of your transactions, and it takes just a couple of clicks to record income and expenditure in your accounts. Even if you've lost a receipt, seeing the transaction there on your bank statement means you're more likely to be able to include it as an expense than if you'd forgotten about that transaction entirely.

The bank feed is enabled through open banking; you connect your bank account by logging into your online banking via your accounting software, which can download transactions into your software as a kind of live bank statement. The idea is that this makes it difficult for any transactions to be missed, unless of course they're not going through the bank account.

Another great thing about the bank feed is that most software will allow you to set up rules which will save you time. For example, to always record expenditure with a certain supplier in the same way. This makes it even quicker to go through the list and record your transactions.

► Invoicing

Accounting software will allow you to raise invoices to your clients really easily. You'll be able to set up invoices from your computer or through the app on your phone and email them to your clients. Some software will enable you to set up automatic reminders if those invoices are overdue, and others will have the option to send reminders to your clients at the touch of a button. You can set up standard products and services with fixed prices, so you don't have to type in the same information every time you send an invoice. Your software will also enable you to see at a glance which of your invoices have been paid or, more importantly, which haven't been paid because the bank feed makes it really simple to match invoices and payments.

► Reporting

One of the features of accounting software which I find most beneficial is the ability to run reports. This is of huge value, both strategically—we'll talk about this in Chapter 7—and operationally. If you're on top of your bookkeeping, you'll be able to run reports which show how much you owe your suppliers, how much is due to you from customers, which customers are paying late, how much profit you made last week, last month or last year, which product or service generated the most income for you…the list is endless!

► Tax position

Knowing your profit will allow you to estimate and budget for your tax bill, and if you're a sole trader using a package designed for sole traders, you may be able to have a view of your tax position at any time. Your software may even be able to submit your self-assessment tax return to HMRC for you.

▶ **VAT**

If you're VAT registered and over the VAT threshold, you'll know that Making Tax Digital (MTD) means that you need to submit your VAT return using MTD-compliant software. We'd never recommend software which isn't MTD-compliant but be aware of this feature. You'll want your software to be able to prepare your VAT return and calculate your VAT bill as you go through each quarter, with the ability to submit that return directly from the software once the quarter end is reached.

▶ **Payroll**

Some accounting systems have an inbuilt payroll function or offer it as an add-on. If you're an employer, this could be a useful feature, but it is also acceptable to run payroll in a separate system (or have somebody run it for you).

"Can't I just use a spreadsheet?"

I'm often asked for a spreadsheet which clients can use to record their income and expenditure. I know that plenty of bookkeeping and accounting firms provide spreadsheets like this because they know that small businesses, especially when starting out, are reluctant to spend money on software. And why do they offer it for free? I'll let you in on a little secret. It means that they can get their smallest clients to put their records into a standard format, making it quicker to do things like produce tax returns, and clients are also less likely to come to them with bags of receipts to sort out in the run up to January 31st, the self-assessment deadline.

At But the Books we've decided not to offer a spreadsheet. Don't get me wrong, I LOVE spreadsheets; we use spreadsheets to do a lot of planning and analysis for our clients. However, as the tool for recording your transactions, we think an accounting system is so much better.

Here are some of the reasons why business owners resist using software and my response to each of those concerns:

» *All I need is a list of income and expenditure*

When starting out, lots of businesses keep a list of sales and a list of expenses, which is fine for the smallest of businesses. However, it makes any kind of analysis more tricky; you might want to identify your biggest customer, confirm which class you run is the most popular, or know how much you spent on advertising last month. If you're familiar with spreadsheets, you'll probably know some formulae which can help you get this information out of your lists, but all of these extras and work-arounds quickly get complicated. This could mean that you spend much more time on your spreadsheet than you want to or perhaps you might even lose interest in keeping it up to date.

Spreadsheets are also prone to manual error. It's easy to type something into your spreadsheet incorrectly or to enter a formula for a total which doesn't pick up the right range of cells and I've seen this happen a couple of times on the spreadsheets used by our clients to prepare their tax returns. They thought their income or expenditure was one figure but, when reviewing their file, I found that actually several transactions, or in one case several months' worth of transactions, had been missed. Errors like this can lead you to misunderstand vital numbers in your business accounts.

» *I'll never be able to understand an accounting system*

If you can use a spreadsheet, you can most likely get your head around the features of a piece of software. In fact, I think the good ones are easier to understand because the areas of your business, like 'sales', 'bank' and 'taxes', are clearly labelled and laid out for you. It's more obvious what you need to input, whereas a spreadsheet is a blank canvas for which you need to decide what to record and how you're going to record it.

» *I don't have enough transactions to need to bother with an accounting system*

That may be so, but if you start using it from day one when you don't have many transactions, you'll already have a good understanding of how the software works when things get busier for you and your business.

Accounting software has changed since the days when a finance person sat in the corner of the office with secret software which only they could touch. Accounting software is now on the cloud and can be accessed on your phone, and your bookkeeper or accountant can log in remotely to give you a hand. It's easy to use (with a bit of training) and it gives you really useful information at the click of a button.

» *I can't afford yet another subscription*

You might be favouring a spreadsheet because it's free, but accounting software is very affordable too; there are even some free packages out there. You can sign up for basic accounting software—suitable for a sole trader—for less than £10 per month, and most of the large software providers offer free trials or discounts at the beginning, giving you the opportunity to find the software package which best works for you.

The cold, hard truth is that if your business can't afford a small expense for a critical function—finance—you should consider whether your business is a business at all.

Which accounting package is right for you?

So, hopefully you're convinced that accounting software is the way forward and you know which features you're looking for, but which package do you choose?

The most important factor behind this decision will be how well a system suits your business needs. But, as you'll find, all of the major software providers have tried to build something which will suit most businesses, so unless you have some very specific requirements, several options will be available to you. The accounting package you choose will also come down to personal preference (i.e. which system you like the look and functionality of the most), so you'll need to do some research and maybe try a free trial of one or two before you're sure which one to go with.

There are four main players in the small business accounting software market: QuickBooks, Xero, FreeAgent and Sage. There are also some lesser-known options, including KashFlow, FreshBooks, Clear Books, Zoho Books and Wave.

When deciding which of these is right for you, you should first consider which features you will need from your software.

Ask yourself the following and these questions will help you narrow down your options:

- » *Are you a sole trader, limited company or something else?*

- » *Are you selling services, products or both?*

- » *Will you have dealings overseas? If so, will you need to work in more than one currency?*

- » *Are you VAT registered?*

- » *Do you have people on payroll?*

- » *Do you need to break down your sales into categories, for example, by region or type of project?*

▶ **For the freelancers**

If you're working alone as a freelancer and you're set up as a sole trader—you might even be running your business as a side hustle around your day job—the best software for you will be one which is set up specifically for sole traders.

The two packages we like are FreeAgent and QuickBooks Self-Employed. Each of these packages will allow you to send invoices to your clients by email, connect your bank account so that you can easily see your income and expenditure, and calculate your tax position. This means that it will either give you the figures to include in your tax return or actually allow you to submit your self-assessment return via the software without needing to log into HMRC's website, Government Gateway, to do it.

▶ **For product-based businesses**

If you're selling a product, you'll want to keep track of how much you have in stock, so software which tracks inventory will be key. It is possible to track stock in a spreadsheet and to record manually the cost of stock sold per month, but we think that software with this functionality built in is worth paying for. You'll also want to be sure that your software works seamlessly with the payment service you've chosen.

We like Xero for product-based businesses because of the ability to track stock. At But the Books we see Xero as a market leader and the team at Xero are trying to stay ahead of their competitors as forerunners in the market by using innovative technology. Ultimately, Xero is by far the most used amongst new clients who come to us with accounting software already in place.

▶ **For service-based businesses**

If you sell services, you'll have no stock to track but it's likely that you're sending a high number of invoices to your clients and you may also be incurring expenses as you travel around to complete various jobs.

Invoicing and keeping track of who has and hasn't paid you is straightforward in any of the packages that we recommend to our clients. Staying on top of expenses can be a bit more complicated and you might choose to use software which integrates with your accounting system, such as Receiptbank or Autoentry. Alternatively, software like QuickBooks and Xero have an expenses function built into their mobile apps, which can be useful for keeping track of receipts on the go.

▶ The free option

Start-ups are often reluctant to pay for anything which seems unnecessary, which is why we see so many businesses keeping their accounts in spreadsheets. There are lots of reasons to pay for software, but there are also free options if you want to use accounting software without the cost.

Wave is free software which does all of the basic things you'd expect from an accounting package. It has an automated bank feed, you can send professional-looking invoices, and you can keep track of who's paid you. You can run reports on aspects of your business, and there are some additional features like payroll which you can add on at a cost. Wave makes its money by taking a commission if you take card payments through the software, which is something to keep in mind.

You might outgrow it faster than some other software packages out there, but if you're a cash-strapped start-up, using Wave is a better alternative to trying to manage with a spreadsheet.

A word on pricing

You need to make sure you're choosing software with the right features for your business. It's not always necessary to have every single feature, so you might find that you can save money by selecting an entry-level version of the software rather than the pro version on day one (but be sure you're selecting software which can grow with you as your business does).

Should you pay for accounting software?

Without a doubt the answer to this question is yes. Software will help you stay on top of your invoicing, understand how your business is doing, keep track of your stock, help you estimate your tax bill, save you time, and give you peace of mind. Let me elaborate on each of the reasons why I think you should consider paying for accounting software.

► **Staying on top of invoicing**

Most software will allow you to set up and email an invoice to your clients from your computer or an app, and because your software also has sight of your bank statement, it's easy to match income against those invoices. The wonderful thing about this is that you can keep track of which customers have and haven't paid you by running a simple report. If you've ever raised invoices using a Word document template and have to check your bank statement every now and again to see who has and hasn't paid you, you'll find this a huge time saver, particularly if you raise a number of invoices every month.

► **Estimating your tax bill**

If you're self-employed and using QuickBooks Self-Employed or FreeAgent's Self-Employed software, you'll have an estimate of the tax you owe as you go through the year which is incredibly helpful for budgeting for your tax bill.

► **Ultimately, it's about time saved and peace of mind**

For me, accounting software is a must. I'll rarely recommend that somebody carries on with a spreadsheet-based system. There is usually a small cost involved but once you know how the system works and get into a routine, you'll see that there is a huge cost saving of your time every month as you tackle your bookkeeping in the future. If nothing else, you won't find yourself returning to a bag-of-receipts accounting method.

I think if you're still undecided, taking a free trial is the way to go. You just don't know what you're missing until you give it a try.

Client story — Sarah

When I first met Sarah, her café had been open for a year. She's a sole trader and she'd called us for help because she needed to prepare her self-assessment return but she'd never done any bookkeeping.

After our phone call I expected this job to be a complex and messy one. We love a challenge after all, but I was right. When we met in person and collected her records, we were faced with boxes of receipts and till readings. Receipts had been stuffed in with no effort to order them, not even by month, some till readings were missing, the till wasn't always cashed up at the end of the day and the owner had been paying for various expenses on her personal card and taking money out of the till to reimburse herself.

This situation isn't unusual, but it is probably the worst I've seen. Apart from the obvious concern that her figures might not be accurate for her tax return, she might have lost paperwork or forgotten to record a transaction. I was also concerned about her ability to run the business and make decisions without any information about how the business was doing financially. Without maintaining an accurate bookkeeping process, how could she possibly know whether she was profitable from month to month or whether it was worth buying more stock?

Sarah acknowledged that bookkeeping wasn't her strong point and appointed us to get her records up to date and prepare monthly bookkeeping for her going forward. Promptly, we set her up with Xero and started making our way through that backlog of transactions so that we could prepare and submit Sarah's tax return, and Sarah could finally see how profitable the shop was on a daily, weekly, monthly and annual basis.

Summary

In this chapter we've discussed the benefits of software over spreadsheets, particularly the way in which accounting software can offer vital insights into how your business is doing. We've also looked at whether you should pay for accounting software and which packages we'd recommend depending on the type of business you're running. I hope it's now obvious to you how worthwhile accounting software can be and how it can transform your bookkeeping, making your life a whole lot easier.

CHAPTER 5
HOW TO DEAL WITH YOUR BAG OF RECEIPTS

Client story — Will

Will sells prints online. He started his business six months before we met him and he hadn't been keeping any accounting records. He contacted us because he was preparing to complete a self-assessment tax return for the first time and needed to know his numbers.

Most of his income came through PayPal via his own website, but he also sold items via a few other websites, receiving his sales proceeds after a commission had been deducted. His costs were mainly art supplies, a little bit of marketing, and postage. Because he was going to the post office almost every day, he had over one hundred post office receipts which he was keeping in a carrier bag. Add to that his receipts for other supplies and invoices he'd received for online purchases—which he'd left in his inbox, not printing them out or saving them anywhere—and you can see why the idea of setting up an accounting system was an overwhelming task for him.

We approached his bag of receipts in our usual logical way and set up his accounting system over a couple of days, providing him with a process which he could follow going forward.

As we discussed in Chapter 2, if you find yourself in a position where you've got a bag of receipts and you don't know where to start, your accounts can become quite an emotional matter. Not knowing how to get started can be stressful, and the feeling that you've left it too long and you'll never be able to get up to date leaves some of our clients feeling embarrassed; it leaves others with a feeling of panic.

Of course, nobody should ever feel embarrassed. Believe me, we've seen everything, and to us it's just a problem to solve. But I can also tell you what an incredible sense of relief our clients have felt once their accounting system is in place. So if you're faced with a bag of receipts right now, put some time in your diary, book out a whole day—maybe two—and work through these steps to get your accounting system set up because it's all about that feeling you get when you're on top of things.

In this chapter we're going to talk about the best time to do this, the best way to file your receipts and the steps to follow to set up your accounting system.

Choosing the best time to set up accounting software

If you're not already using accounting software, I'd really recommend looking into setting this up as soon as possible. From Chapter 4, you'll know that I rarely recommend that anybody sticks with a spreadsheet, and even if you're a real whizz with Excel and have incredible self-discipline, you're missing out on a lot of insight into how your business is doing if you're not using accounting software. If you start now, you can record your transactions for the current financial year, start understanding your business better from today and run the reports you need when your year end arrives.

You're going to need to decide on a date for when your accounting records start in your accounting software. The most sensible start date is the start of the financial year; if you're a sole trader this is April 6th, and if you run a limited company it's the first day of your financial year. If it's already a long way into the financial year, don't let that put you off. You could keep six months' worth of your records in a spreadsheet—if that's what you were using previously—and then the records for the rest of the financial year in your accounting software. The important thing is to choose your start date and to get started. Just be careful to ensure that you don't duplicate any transactions.

If you've been using another piece of accounting software previously, perhaps a free package which you've now outgrown and you want to set up a new system, I'd recommend sticking with your old software until the end of your financial year, and using the year-end date as your switching date. You might feel impatient, but I've worked with businesses which have switched part way through the year and it can cause a headache if you're not really on top of things, not least because if you try to run any reports, half of your year is recorded in one system and half is recorded in another.

If you can't wait, I'd suggest picking a month-end date and switching on that date. You'll need to work very closely with a bookkeeper or accountant to make sure you don't miss or duplicate any transactions over the switching period and that your opening balances are correct in the new system, accurately reflecting, for example, which customer invoices are outstanding.

Setting up your accounting system

So, you've decided to set up an accounting system. You've done your research and chosen the system which is right for you and your business. You've signed up, and you've decided on the date to make the switch. What next?

✓ Set up your chart of accounts

Your chart of accounts is the list of categories you'll use to record your transactions; in accounting jargon we often call these 'codes' or 'accounts'. Each type of income, expense, asset or liability has its own unique code, meaning that similar transactions can be grouped together and fed into the correct location in your financial statements.

Most accounting systems have a pre-defined chart of accounts and it's usually absolutely fine to use them as they come. For example, your new accounting system might be set up to record sales against code 101, material costs against 201, and transport costs against 250. If you want to customise your chart of accounts, now's a great time to do it. Let's say you run a greeting cards business and you want to divide your sales into birthday cards, Valentine's cards and wedding day cards; you might choose to set up codes 102, 103 and 104 to record your sales in this level of detail.

✓ Connect your bank account

The wonderful thing about having an accounting system is that you can connect your business bank account. All of your bank transactions will feed into your accounting system and you can run through the list and record each of them in just a couple of clicks. (Honestly, you'll wonder why it took you so long to make the leap into the world of accounting software!) Connect your bank account now and leave the days of paper bank statements in the past.

Usually, when you first connect a bank account, only up to the past three months of transactions will be pulled into your software. If your switching date is before this, you'll need to pull in other bank transactions manually. However, this is straightforward, with most software simply requiring you to download a .csv file of your bank statement from your online banking and uploading it using a template into your accounting software. Your software's help section will talk you through how to do this.

✓ Enter your opening balances

You'll need to enter your opening balances at the switching date and for this to make sense, you'll need to understand a few accounting basics (see Chapter 6). But for now, what you need to know is that your business's income and expenditure build up over the course of a year, giving you a net profit or loss figure at the year end. When you reach the end of the year, everything resets, and you start afresh from zero.

If you're starting to use your accounting system from the start of a financial year, you'll need to know the value of your assets and liabilities and your equity. Assets and liabilities—things the business owns and owes, like bank balances, stock and machinery, and balances owed by customers and owed to suppliers—roll over from year to year, as does what we call equity, what the business is worth. If you're starting midway through a year, you'll need to know these, plus any income and expenditure which has been incurred in the financial year to date.

This can get a bit technical and I'd recommend speaking to a bookkeeper or accountant if you're not sure.

✓ **Set up customers and suppliers**

At this point, you might choose to spend some time setting up each of your suppliers in your accounting software, recording their names, addresses and terms. Some businesses find that it's easier to do this all in one go, but others prefer just to skip forward to using the software and to set up suppliers and customers as and when a transaction with that contact occurs. Choose whichever you think you'll find easiest – it's up to you.

✓ **Set up products and standard pricing**

If you have products which you sell with set prices, it's worth setting these up in your software at the start. This will save you time when raising invoices because once each product or service is set up, you can select it from a list and your invoice will populate with the price, the account code you want to use to track the sale and the VAT rate if applicable, meaning that you won't have to enter the details manually each time.

✓ **Start using your system**

Once you've followed these steps, you'll be able to start using your accounting system. Get into good habits and record those bank transactions regularly and you'll be amazed at how much easier it is to understand your business accounts.

The best way to file receipts

When I started working as a freelance bookkeeper, I used to work from home. One of my clients told me that her husband was going to drop off her receipts one evening and when he arrived I was bathing my daughter so my husband answered the door. When he came upstairs to tell me the client's receipts had arrived, he said, "There are a lot!" I was expecting *a lot* of receipts, but I never could have expected quite as many as there were.

My husband told me that my client's partner had apologised sheepishly, clearly a little embarrassed. Thinking back to that day and how that client might have been feeling, I can see perhaps why she'd asked somebody else to deliver the receipts on her behalf. I expect that she was worried because they weren't particularly well organised, that some might be missing, and that some of them were dated so long ago that she might not quite remember what they were all for. Of course, the size of the job didn't faze me at all, and that's because I've seen it all before; but I can understand how bad the client must have been feeling, why her husband felt he needed to apologise, and why my husband was a bit shocked.

For any business, the goal is to keep your paperwork nicely organised. This will save you a lot of time if you're doing your own books and a lot of money (in terms of time) if you're outsourcing your bookkeeping to a bookkeeper or accountant.

✓   Record and file your receipts immediately

It takes discipline, but the best way to stay on top of your receipts is to record them straight away. Receipts are often lost when you're out and about, so I suggest using your phone to take a photo of a receipt the moment you're handed one. Ideally, you'll upload your receipt directly into your accounting system through the app, something which is really straightforward to do. But if you don't fancy this, your software doesn't offer that function or this is just one step too far, you could take photos on your phone and keep them in a special folder named 'Receipts' or something equally catchy.

If you're the kind of person who'd rather deal with your receipts once a week or once a month, you might find it helpful to keep an envelope in your bag or your car or wherever you're most likely to be when you incur business expenses. Then, you can pop the receipt in there and avoid losing it. Although this method will reduce the risk of you losing a receipt, beware that this strategy is a risky one if you tend to procrastinate on your bookkeeping, as it could lead to the big bag of receipts you want to avoid.

✓   Organise your receipts by date

Whether you're doing your own books or paying a bookkeeper or accountant to do them for you, more than likely you or they are working through your accounts chronologically every week or month. A receipt or invoice will be needed to back up your transactions and, as your transactions feed into your accounting software from your bank statement one day at a time, it makes sense to keep your receipts organised by date.

One method which works well for clients is to keep one folder for each calendar month (or week if they have heaps of transactions). This means that if you are prone to leaving your bookkeeping to a rainy day in 8 months' time, at least it will be fairly easy to find the receipts which match the transactions on your statement as you work through them. There's nothing worse than trying to find a specific Staples receipt when you've been shopping there 40 times in the past year.

✓ Don't worry about suppliers too much

Sometimes, I see clients filing receipts by supplier, but I'd rather see receipts filed by date. This is simply because when I work through a client's bank statement, I start with their oldest transactions and work forwards to the present day. It's quicker for me to locate a receipt for June if it's in a 'June' folder. If your records are kept by supplier, I'll constantly be opening and closing files as I work through your transactions, which will take much longer than it needs to. By all means, file your receipts by supplier within your month folder if you have so many transactions that this feels worthwhile, but recording by supplier first and then by month can be a bit of a headache. If all else fails, though, just use a consistent filing method.

✓ Write on your receipts

Write on your receipts what the spending was for. That way, when you give them to your bookkeeper, it will save time as they'll know how to record the expense. Also, if some of the spending on the receipts was a personal cost, cross out the item.

✓ Request VAT receipts

If you're VAT registered, you must have a VAT receipt or VAT invoice for expenses you wish to claim in your VAT return. Make sure you request a VAT receipt or VAT invoice for every purchase. A mistake our clients often make is to keep just the card receipt for transactions—which doesn't contain any detail about VAT—without the full itemised till receipt, which makes it impossible to know what they bought.

✓ Make the most of available software

If you really have got a lot of receipts and not a lot of time or patience to organise them, you might like to look at software like ReceiptBank or AutoEntry which integrate with the main accounting packages. They incur a small cost, but this small investment can be so valuable when you have a lot of transactions to process quickly. It's easy: first, you take a photo of your receipts via the app on your phone. The software then reads data from the receipts and transfers that information to your accounting system. In a few clicks you can then match transactions from your bank feed against the transactions on your receipts, requiring minimal data entry from you.

Once you've taken a photo of those receipts and they're successfully logged in your accounting system, you're free to throw them away, no need to spend time filing.

Summary

In this chapter we've looked at the best time to set up an accounting system, the steps you need to follow in order to set up said system, and how to file your receipts so that you can find the one you need when recording your transactions. If you're somebody who just likes to get stuck into things, hopefully this has given you the information you need to get started, but if you're less confident or there's anything complex about your business, or if you're changing to new software part way through the year, you may well decide to seek support from a bookkeeper or accountant to help you with this step.

CHAPTER 6
A VERY BRIEF LESSON IN ACCOUNTANCY

I once saw a course advertised which promised to teach you everything you need to know about accountancy in three hours. Given that I took four years to qualify as an accountant, I took extra exams to earn the business's bookkeeping license and I need to embark on new training courses each time I want But the Books to offer a new service, I feel that this promise was hugely misleading.

Bookkeeping and accounting are not things you can learn in three hours and I'm not even going to try to cover everything; however, I can teach you some of the basics. It's impossible to get your bookkeeping right if you have no grasp of how accounting works so we'll start with the basic principles. These are the concepts which you should always have in mind. We'll talk about timing and when to record transactions, we'll look at the different accounting reports you need to know about and how these are affected by different transactions and, finally, we'll look at some common pitfalls where we often see clients recording things incorrectly.

A basic foundation will allow you to record the majority of your transactions without mishap, but undoubtedly something will crop up where you'll need more support. You've got a few options here: you can read up on accounting some more—your accounting software provider will often have help articles addressing common, more technical transactions— or to engage a professional who can help with the more complicated things, and in Chapter 11 I'll talk you through how to find a great bookkeeper.

Client story – Richard

Richard came to us because he was struggling to make sense of the figures he was seeing in his accounting system. He'd been doing his own books for the past three years but didn't have a financial background.

At the end of the financial year, Richard's accountant prepared and filed his year-end accounts for him by using and adjusting data from Richard's accounting system. The problem for Richard was that the year-end accounts shared with Companies House didn't reflect the financial records he had made via his accounting software.

This is when he came to But The Books and we spent several days making sense of his accounting records and tweaking them accordingly. Richard could have saved a lot of money (in terms of our time) by finding out how to record things correctly or employing somebody with the right knowledge and experience from day one.

Accounting fundamentals

Here are some fundamental accounting principles which you need to understand in order to record transactions for your business correctly. As a business owner, you are responsible for making sure that your accounts are free from error and if at any point you're unsure or things get more complex than you're able to deal with, you should hire a professional to help you.

▶ **Consistency**

The first rule, or accounting concept, is consistency. Once you've decided on a method for recording transactions, you should use the same method for every transaction of its type every time and every year. You are allowed to change the method—we call it an 'accounting policy'—but only if there's a good reason, and once you've decided on your accounting policy, you need to stick with it.

An example of where consistency might come into play is with valuing stock. There are a number of different ways to decide how much your stock is worth and we'll talk about this in more detail at the end of the chapter. In short, however, it's important to use a consistent method of stock valuation, otherwise your stock's value could differ between transactions, making it impossible to calculate your profits accurately.

► **Prudence**

The next rule is what accountants call the 'prudence concept', which means the most conservative position is recorded for every transaction so that 1) you don't overestimate your business's income, assets and profits and 2) you don't underestimate your costs, liabilities and losses.

In practice, this means that you can only record transactions when they are very likely to happen. For example, you can't include income in your accounts when your client hasn't even approved the quote. A stock-related example is that items need to be valued at the lowest possible sale price (we call this net present value in the accounting world) and the original cost. If the amount you paid for an item is higher than the amount you could now sell it for—perhaps because it has perished in some way or it's now unfashionable and has therefore lost value—and you value it at cost, you're overstating the value of your assets. This is because when you come to sell it, it's not going to recover as much as the figure you've stated in your accounts.

► **Accruals**

Finally, you should be aware of the 'accruals concept'. This is about recording transactions in the financial period in which they took place and not necessarily when the cash exchanged hands. The accruals concept is an important one in accounting; limited companies must use it and it can be used by sole traders, although smaller sole traders have the option to record transactions using what we call 'cash basis' instead—recording income and expenditure as and when it is received or paid out—if they wish, which some business owners find more convenient.

▶ **Cash basis vs accruals basis**

If you've already completed a self-assessment tax return and your turnover is under the VAT threshold (which at the time of publishing is £85,000), you may have seen a box which asks whether you are preparing your accounts using the cash basis.

Very small businesses are allowed to use cash-basis accounting, meaning that they can record their transactions using the date when the cash went in or out of their bank account. This makes it much more straightforward for small businesses who aren't always up to date with their bookkeeping to prepare their self-assessment accounts because they can simply run through their bank statement to see which transactions happened during the financial year and use these figures to work out their profit.

Larger businesses aren't able to use this method. They need to apply the accruals concept and record their transactions using the dates upon which the transaction was deemed to take place, i.e. the date of an invoice, which is not necessarily when the cash changed hands.

Let's say you're a consultant and you invoice a client for some completed work on March 30th. Under the accruals concept, that transaction took place on March 30th, but if your client doesn't pay until April 20th, under the cash basis the transaction took place on April 20th. This may not seem very significant as the client only took a few weeks to pay. However, if you're preparing your year-end accounts up to March 31st or April 5th, the transaction would fall into a different financial year depending on whether it was made under the accruals basis or cash basis. It is important to be aware of which method you are using and to apply it consistently, paying particular attention to transactions happening around the year end.

Accounting reports

We need accounting reports to see how our business is doing and to prepare our returns to HMRC at the end of each year and to Companies House if we run a limited company. It is also really helpful to be able to run reports throughout the year so that you can see how your business is performing. So, what are the key business reports and what can they tell you about your business?

The two main business reports you really need to know about are the 'Profit and Loss report' (also known as an 'Income Statement') and the 'Balance Sheet'. These are the reports you'll see if you ever open the annual report and accounts for a large business, and they're reports you'll file with Companies House at the end of the year if you run a limited company.

Profit and Loss (P&L) report

This report is about your business's profit. It tells you the value of your sales and expenditure and the profit the business has made during the time the report covers (usually a year). This report is generally run at the year end to cover a full financial year, but you can also run the report to cover the period you're interested in, whether that's the last financial year, this year to date, last month, this month, this quarter or last week.

The precise layout and wording may differ depending on your accounting system, but this is the information you'd expect to see on your P&L report:

✓ **Sales income**

This is the obvious one. You can't make profit without sales, so the first figure you'll see on the P&L report will be the value of your sales within the period.

✓ **Cost of sales**

These are the costs directly associated with making your sales. This could include things like material costs and the cost of staff who are employed purely to produce the product or service that you're selling. In my experience, people often find it difficult to distinguish exactly which costs are their costs of sales and which are their overheads. (More about overheads in a moment.)

Some examples are:

» For a design agency – the cost of hiring a freelance photographer to photograph products for the client's website, the cost of which will be passed on to the client

» For a personal trainer – the cost of hiring another PT to run one of their classes

» For an artist – the cost of a canvas

» For online retailers – the cost of payment charges incurred by third party providers such as PayPal or Stripe

If you're self-employed, your time spent producing goods or delivering a service is never a cost of sale.

✓ **Overheads**

These are all of the business's other costs, i.e. things which can't be linked directly to a specific sale.

Overheads include:

» IT expenses – your software, cloud storage, web hosting and small pieces of IT equipment you buy during the year, such as mice and keyboards

» Rent and service charges (for an office or hot desking)

» Marketing – general advertising, printing business cards, flyers, leaflets and brochures, and networking

» Your phone line and mobile phones

» Subscriptions (including memberships of professional bodies)

» Accounting software

Overheads also include costs for staff which are not considered costs of sales, so whether you have marketing staff, administrative staff or a general manager, their salaries, pensions, costs of training them and any other costs associated with their employment such as travel and expenses will go here. If you hire contractors—virtual assistants, social media managers or a bookkeeper—their costs will be included in overheads, too.

Again, if you're a sole trader, your 'wages' are not included in overheads—they should be recorded as drawings (more about this coming up)—but if your business is a limited company and you're a director taking a salary, your salary is an overhead.

✓ **Profit**

There are two profit figures you'll see on the P&L report. The business's gross profit, which is calculated as sales minus cost of sales, and net profit, which is sales minus cost of sales and overheads.

Your gross profit tells you how profitable the products and/or services your business is selling are. This is important because if what you're selling isn't making a gross profit, you have no hope of covering your overheads and still being profitable. As well as seeing the gross profit for the whole business, your accounting software—if set up correctly—might also list the gross profit individually for the different goods and services you sell.

Net profit shows you overall, after taking into account all other costs, how profitable the business is. As overheads are for the business as a whole and cannot be attributed to different products, the net profit pertains to the whole business.

Balance Sheet

Sales, costs, profit. So far, nothing too complicated, but people often find the concept of a Balance Sheet more mystical. The Balance Sheet is a report which shows you what the business owns and what it owes at any point in time. It can be considered as one way of reviewing the financial health of the business because it shows overall whether the business (and therefore the owners of the business) has more assets than liabilities and is in the black, or whether it owes money to others.

The Balance Sheet gives you a snapshot of your business's financial position on one specific day. It's usually run on the last day of the financial year, but you might want to run it to coincide with the last day of the period for which you're running a P&L report in order to give you a full view of your business. Here's the key information you'd expect to see on your Balance Sheet.

✓ Assets

There are two groups of assets: those to be held for a long time, known as 'fixed assets', and those to be held for a much shorter period, called 'current assets'.

> »   Fixed assets
>
> These are items owned by the business which will be kept for an extended period of time and help the business to generate income – like machines and buildings.
>
> Let's say you're a tailor and you buy a sewing machine for your business which will be used to produce trousers and it is likely to last for five years. It wouldn't be right to record this as an expense in year one because you'd have a high expense figure in that year and no expenses in the next four years. You want your accounts to reflect that a portion of the sewing machine's cost applies to each of the five years. We do this through a process called 'depreciation', which means reducing the value of the asset on the Balance Sheet each year and charging it as an expense to the profit and loss account.
>
> Depreciation can be complex and, confusingly, because depreciation is an adjustment we make for accounting purposes and not a real cost, (depreciation is not allowable for tax) tax rules are different to accounting rules. Sole traders who use the cash basis, for example, are allowed to record the full cost of certain fixed assets as an expense in the year purchased rather than spreading the cost over the life of

the asset. That means sole traders might see that big expense in year 1. Limited companies, on the other hand, use capital allowances to adjust their profits for tax computations, so the approaches are different depending on your business's set-up.

Ultimately, it's important to remember that fixed assets aren't a cost and aren't part of your overheads, depreciation is the amount which is recorded as an overhead; If you have fixed assets and are unsure of what to include in your tax return or year-end accounts, do seek advice from a bookkeeper or accountant.

» Current assets

These are items owned by the business which are transitory, such as cash in the business's bank account, amounts owed to the business by customers—because soon these will be cash in the business's bank account, too—and stock.

✓ Liabilities (long-term and current)

Liabilities are amounts the business owes to other businesses, people and organisations and, as with assets, they are split into two groups depending on their lifespan. Any liabilities which will take more than one year to pay off, such as long-term bank loans, are classed as long-term liabilities. Current liabilities are the items owed by the business which will be paid off in less than one year. This includes things like bank overdrafts, credit card debts, taxes due and amounts owed to suppliers for invoices which haven't yet been paid.

✓ Net Assets

By adding up all the assets of the business and taking away the liabilities, you can see the net assets of the business. Let's say your business has net assets of £10,000. This simply means the business owns £10,000 more than it owes. You can also say that £10,000 is the value which has been built up in the business.

The net assets belong to the shareholders or owners of the business so net assets are a reflection of what their investment in the business is worth.

✓ Equity

The final section you'll see on the Balance Sheet is 'Equity'. This section shows the owner's initial investment in the business (in limited companies this will be listed as 'share capital') plus retained profit in the business and occasionally other reserves. For sole traders this will be owner funds introduced and retained profit, (profit which has been stored up in the business and not paid out to the owners.) Effectively, this section is a summary of how the net assets have been generated, and because in accountancy a Balance Sheet must 'balance'. You'll find that the total of the equity section will match the total of the business's net assets.

Bookkeeping transactions

So, we now have an understanding of the two main reports used in bookkeeping and accounting. In the next section we're going to look at how to record the most commonly experienced transactions and we'll also look at how they affect the P&L report and Balance Sheet.

There are two sides to every story and it's no different in bookkeeping. Bookkeeping relies on a system called 'double-entry bookkeeping', about which a monk called Luca Pacioli published a book in circa 1494. The system is built on the principle that every transaction has two sides to it. If you buy a book, for example, you decrease your bank balance and increase the number of books you own. If you sell a car, you increase your bank balance and decrease the number of cars you own. If you borrow some money, you increase your bank balance and you increase how much money you owe.

In double entry, one side of every transaction generates a debit entry and the other side creates a credit entry. If you've ever been £100 overdrawn and checked your bank balance, you'll probably have seen that your balance is £100DR. This is the bank saying that from its point of view you are in debit to them, or that you are an asset to them as you owe them money.

Some sections of the P&L report and Balance Sheet are debited when they increase and credited when they decrease, and others are credited when they increase and debited when they decrease. To really get to grips with double-entry bookkeeping, you need to remember which categories behave in which way.

▶ **A way to remember debits and credits**

A mnemonic I was taught to remember which transactions result in debits and which ones result in credits is DEAD RELIC: Debits increase Expenses, Assets and Dividends and Revenue, Equity and Liabilities are Increased by Credits. It's a bit of a mouthful but it is a helpful way to remember the rule and might help the next section make a bit more sense.

Category	Definition	Increased by debit or credit
Expense	A cost split into cost of sales and overheads	Debit
Asset	Something owned by the business	Debit
Dividend	A distribution of company profit to shareholders	Debit
Revenue	Income earned by the business	Credit
Equity	Share capital and profits retained in the business	Credit
Liability	An amount owed by the business	Credit

People find the idea of debits and credits complex (even bookkeepers and accountants have to think it through sometimes) so don't get too hung up on this. Your accounting system will do the work for you; it is just worth explaining because it will help you understand what's happening to your accounting reports each time you record a transaction.

✓ Recording a sale

When you make a sale, you increase your sales figure (credit revenue) – you'll see this in your P&L report, and increase the money you have in cash or in your bank account which will appear on your Balance Sheet (debit asset).

If you make your sale by raising an invoice to your customer, you still increase your sales figure in your P&L account (credit revenue) but the other side of the transaction is that you increase the money owed to your business, known as your 'debtors' or 'accounts receivable' on your Balance Sheet (debit asset). When that customer pays and settles their invoice, you decrease your debtors (credit asset) and increase your money in the bank (debit asset).

Note, of course, that if you're a sole trader using the cash basis, you will never have debtors in your Balance Sheet because the sale is only recorded when the money goes into your bank account.

✓ Recording expenditure

When you incur an expense, you increase expenditure on your P&L account (debit expense) and decrease the money you have in cash or in your bank account, which will appear on your Balance Sheet (credit asset).

If your supplier invoices you rather than you paying by cash or card, you increase your expenditure figure in your P&L account (debit expense) and you increase the money owed to your supplier, known as your 'creditors' or 'accounts payable' in your Balance Sheet (credit liability). When you pay your supplier to settle their invoice, you decrease the amount owed to your creditors (debit liability) and decrease your money in the bank account (credit asset).

Again, if you're a sole trader using the cash basis, you will never have creditors in your Balance Sheet because the purchase is only recorded when the money goes out of your bank account.

✓ Buying an asset

As you'll remember, assets are not recorded as expenses in the P&L; instead, they're recorded on the Balance Sheet. If you buy a sewing machine, for example, you'll increase your assets (debit asset) and decrease your bank balance (credit asset).

At the end of every year, you'll record a transaction to reflect how much of that asset has been used up in the year (depreciation). We do that by recording an expense in the P&L report (debit expense) and reducing the value of the asset on the Balance Sheet (credit asset).

✓ Lending money to the business

When you start a business it's likely that you'll pay some costs on behalf of the business from your own pocket or that you'll lend the business a lump sum of cash.

If you pay for some expenses on behalf of the business, you will record those expenses in your P&L (debit expense) just as you would if they'd been paid directly from the business bank account, but rather than crediting the business's bank account, you'll record a liability to yourself if you run a limited company (credit liability) or funds introduced (credit equity) if you're a sole trader.

On the day when the business repays the loans you've made to it, this will be recorded to reflect the decrease in the business bank account (credit asset), removing the funds owed to you (debit liability).

Phew! That was a lot of jargon, so feel free to go and make a cuppa before we carry on.

Things people get wrong

We're often engaged by clients to review their accounts and bookkeeping. Frequently, the client has been trading for a while, doing their own bookkeeping, and has reached a point where things are getting complex and they need an expert to cast their eye over the records. We see a few common errors and the next section covers these mistakes so that you can avoid making them.

▶ **Sole trader drawings**

As explained in Chapter 3, when you're a sole trader, you and your business are legally the same entity. This means that the money in your business's bank account is your money. If you 'pay yourself' an amount from that bank account each month, all this really means is that you're moving money from one of your bank accounts to another. The 'wage' you're paying yourself is not an expense of the business.

The bank balance decreases (credit asset), but rather than recording an expense (debit expense) which we often see clients doing, you should increase drawings (debit equity).

▶ **Payroll**

If you employ staff, it's essential to record the payroll transactions properly. If you're running payroll through your accounting software then your payroll transactions should be posted correctly automatically, but if you're employing somebody else to do your payroll or if you're using another tool to do it, you'll need to manually record the payroll transactions in your accounting software each payday and we often see businesses failing to do this.

An employee's gross pay—the cost to the business of that individual's salary—is not the amount the employee will actually receive. One must take into account various deductions, such PAYE tax, National Insurance (NI) and employees' pension contributions (and, for some, student loan repayments or workplace benefits). As an employer, you'll have other additional costs relating to employer pension contributions and employers' National Insurance.

On occasion, I've seen clients accounting for salaries as one lump sum figure as if the only accounting entries are to decrease the bank balance (credit asset) and increase the salary expense (debit expenses). Of course, this is incorrect as it fails to record the many different elements of salaries, so let me talk you through how staff costs should be recorded:

»   **Gross pay** – this is the cost to the business of your employee and it increases your salary expenses for the year (debit expense) and creates a liability for you to pay your employee (credit liability).

»   **PAYE** – this is an amount you deduct from the employee's salary and pay to HMRC, thus reducing the amount payable to the employee (debit liability), but also creating a different liability to pay HMRC instead (credit liability).

»   **Employers' NI** – this is an expense to the business (debit expense) and creates a liability to pay NI to HMRC (credit liability).

»   **Employees' NI** – this is another amount deducted from the employee's salary, thus reducing the net pay which is due to the employee (debit liability) but creating a liability to pay NI to HMRC (credit liability).

»   **Employers' pension** – this is an expense to the business (debit expense) and it creates a liability to pay the pension provider (credit liability).

»   **Employees' pension** – this is deducted from the employee's salary (debit liability) to pay to the pension provider (credit liability).

»   **Net pay** – this is the amount due to your employee and the balancing figure when adding up all the ins and outs in your employee's payslip and on the 'wages payable' liability code on your Balance Sheet. When wages are paid, the double entry is to decrease the bank balance (credit asset) and to debit the liability.

This might seem like a lot of entries and there may be others depending on which deductions your employees need to have made from their salaries, but it is necessary to post each of the entries in order to account for your payroll correctly.

Work out whether something belongs on your P&L or your Balance Sheet and ask yourself whether the transaction is an expense of the business or a liability to pay somebody.

▶ **Stock**

We frequently see mistakes with the bookkeeping for stock. Items purchased should be recorded as a cost of sale (debit purchases, credit bank), but a year-end adjustment must be made to reflect stock which hasn't been sold at the year end.

If you buy 100 of an item but only sell 60 of them during the year, to account for 100 as a cost to your business would understate your profits which would be incorrect. It would also mean you'd incorrectly accounted for the assets the business held at the year end.

Once a stock-take has been performed, an adjustment should be made to credit cost of sales and debit stock on the Balance Sheet. To have an even more accurate view of profits and the Balance Sheet position, most businesses perform stock-takes and post these adjustments monthly or quarterly rather than wait until the end of the year.

Summary

In this chapter we've looked at the fundamental concepts of accounting which you should keep in mind when doing your bookkeeping. We've looked at the difference between the accruals basis and the cash basis which will ensure that you account for your transactions in the right time period. We've looked at the two main accounting reports: the Profit and Loss report, which tells you about your business performance for the year or any term of your choice, and the Balance Sheet, which tells you about what the business owns and owes.

We've looked at some of the main bookkeeping transactions, how to record them and what effect each will have on your P&L report and Balance Sheet so you can start to make sense of debits and credits.

Of course, all of this is quite technical and if you're struggling to make sense of it all, just can't get your head around double entry or aren't sure how to record your transactions, then I urge you to engage a bookkeeper or accountant to help you with your accounts.

Now that we've covered how to record your transactions correctly, we'll look at how to set up a regular bookkeeping process for your business which you can follow and maintain.

CHAPTER 7
A REGULAR PROCESS TO FOLLOW GOING FORWARD

So, you've started your business. You've decided on a legal structure, you've opened a separate bank account, you've set up an accounting system, you know enough about bookkeeping to record your transactions correctly, and you've dealt with your bag of receipts. Now you need to make sure that you can stay on top of it all. And the way to do that is to have a regular process to follow.

The idea of having a regular bookkeeping process might not make your heart sing. But, just think back to Chapter 1 when you considered your motivation for having up-to-date records. Having this at the front of your mind will help you decide on and commit to keeping up with your new process. What we find is that people have good intentions but, just like anybody embarking on a new fitness regime, it doesn't happen unless you create opportunities for your new habits to form.

Client story — Emma

Emma runs a clothing business. She's VAT registered and when she came to us it was close to the deadline for filing her latest VAT return, but she hadn't completed her bookkeeping. She told us that every quarter had been the same. She didn't know where to start with her books, so she put it off until just before the deadline and then had a rush to get everything completed, often having to dedicate a whole weekend to sorting her books.

Emma wasn't ready to outsource her full bookkeeping process, but she hired us to do a quarterly review of her books, meaning she does her own bookkeeping and we review her accounting records to check that the bookkeeping is correct. We also gave Emma a monthly checklist which she follows each time she brings her books up to date. This removes that overwhelming sense of defeat because now she knows where to start. The accountability of knowing that she has a quarterly review meeting is also a motivator to keep her books up to date and Emma's now in an better place all round, with no more weekends lost to bookkeeping.

"What's a simple bookkeeping process I can follow?"

Our new clients are often looking for help with establishing a simple system which they can use throughout the year so that they don't leave all of their bookkeeping until tax return season, their year-end filing deadline or, like Emma, their VAT deadline. These clients have usually just been through a messy and stressful year end because their accounts weren't up to date and they had to do a whole year's bookkeeping at the last minute to get their accounts filed or their tax return submitted. We help them set up an accounting system if they don't already have one, we deal with their bags of receipts and then we either take on their regular bookkeeping or we hand over to them a straightforward process they can follow.

So, let's look at what a bookkeeping system looks like and how you can implement something which you know you'll stick to from month to month.

✓ Make time for bookkeeping

The first step in having a regular bookkeeping process is to ensure you have time available to do it. Book time in your diary regularly, whether monthly, fortnightly or weekly, to do your bookkeeping and make it a non-negotiable appointment.

For some of our monthly bookkeeping clients, we schedule half a day per fortnight or a few hours once per week so that we can stay on top of things and keep things moving along. For some clients we may need to do just an hour of bookkeeping per week, with a longer session at the end of the month in the busier week when payroll is run or month-end figures need finalising.

Scheduling regular time to keep things moving along avoids any build-up of transactions and ensures that important bills and tasks aren't missed. Taking this approach also means that you don't feel like you have to be logged into your accounting system all the time in case you miss anything because you know that at worst your invoicing, supplier invoices and banking were last reviewed no more than seven days ago.

✓ **Use a system that works for you**

As covered in Chapter 4, we almost always recommend that clients set up an accounting system. I really do think it's the best way to keep your records and it gives you a lot more functionality than just using a spreadsheet. I know that some people find new systems and technology confusing and that this might put them off wanting to do their books. If that's the case, do consider whether bookkeeping is something you might be better outsourcing. If for budget reasons outsourcing is out of the question at the moment, then you need to come up with a system that works for you, have a process that you follow each and every time, and stick with it.

✓ **Have a checklist**

I'm a huge fan of checklists. We use them for our client work to ensure that nothing gets missed in our monthly routines. Every business is slightly different but there are tasks which need to be done each week or month like recording sales, whether this is invoicing for your consultancy business or recording cash takings from your market stall.

A bookkeeping checklist

If you'd like to, you can build your own checklist based on the rest of this chapter, or you can head to the back of the book and take our pre-written Monthly Finance Checklist as a starting point.

You might also find it helpful to write a process note for your bookkeeping, particularly if you're somebody for whom bookkeeping doesn't come as second nature and you're worried that you'll forget the steps you need to follow from one week to the next.

When we set up accounting systems for our clients, we always give them a list of tasks they need to do regularly alongside a guide on the more complicated things. This means that when they do their bookkeeping they can just start at the top of the list and work through it, referring to the process note for the things they find complex. We also like to give them a quick reference guide of the codes used in their accounting system and the suppliers who generally get recorded against these codes. This saves time when you're deciding whether your payment to QuickBooks should be recorded under software or accounting fees, for example.

Invoicing

Invoicing should be one of your priorities every time you look at your business bookkeeping. Making sales is one thing, but for people to pay you, you need to raise invoices for your work. Some people feel nervous about sending invoices and procrastinate about doing it, but if you've agreed your payment terms (whether that's 30-day terms, 14-day terms, etc.), by delaying invoicing you're simply adding more and more time to those terms. The first step in ensuring timely payments from your customers is to actually raise your invoices.

I'd suggest sending invoices out as soon as a piece of work is complete. You might need to amend your terms and conditions if this is a change to how you're currently doing it. Depending on your profession, you might even find that there's an opportunity to invoice your clients when the work you've done for them is at draft stage. That's certainly what we do with tax returns. We get to the point where they're drafted, knowing that changes are likely to be minimal and invoice our client when we send them that draft to sign off. It's just an item on our checklist to send the invoice at that point, it's part of the workflow, and it's our guarantee that our client will pay us because we don't complete the job (file the tax return) unless the client settles up.

Building invoicing into your workflow rather than seeing it as a finance activity can certainly help manage this part of your bookkeeping, but if you can't do that, think about which time is best to do your invoicing. Some clients like to raise new invoices daily, but in practice doing your invoicing weekly is manageable for most business owners.

Supplier invoices

No doubt you receive the occasional supplier invoice which you need to pay and these need to be recorded on your accounting system so that you can see which invoices need to be paid at any given time.

You can, of course, add invoices to your system manually, but the most efficient way of recording supplier invoices is to connect an app like ReceiptBank to your accounting system and to remember to send your receipts and supplier invoices through that app every time.

You can upload paperwork to ReceiptBank manually, but in our opinion it's quicker to take photos of physical paperwork using the phone app or forward emails you receive with invoices attached straight to your unique ReceiptBank email address. You might even ask the supplier to 'cc' to that email address when they issue future invoices so that you don't even have to remember to forward it. ReceiptBank works by reading the data on the invoice and populating the fields of a draft purchase invoice in your accounting system. You simply need to check that it has picked up the right data and publish the transaction to your accounting software. It reduces data entry for you and it's a real time saver if you have a lot of supplier invoices.

Pay your suppliers

You might have some supplier invoices which you haven't yet paid. The way to find outstanding invoices is to run an aged payables report, which shows you how much is due to each of your suppliers and how old the debt is. Generally, the report is generated as a table. It shows suppliers down one side and periods along the top to indicate how old each debt is. You'll see current payables which aren't due for payment yet and then payables broken into columns to indicate how overdue they are.

Depending on your software, you can run the report at a summary level which simply shows a list of suppliers and a breakdown of the time period in question, or a detailed report which lists every invoice.

Armed with your aged payables report, you are then in a position to arrange payments, so log into your online banking and get payments set up, scheduling the payments to be made as close to the supplier's due date as you can so as to keep the money in your bank account for as long as possible to strengthen your cash flow and to maximise your ability to earn interest.

Do your banking and review your bank account

In terms of physically doing your banking it's likely that there's little to do, but if you take payments by cash and cheque, you need to pay these into your bank account regularly. You'll also need to spend much more time reviewing transactions which have gone through the bank account and ensuring that they're recorded properly in your accounting system.

It's likely that a few more transactions have gone through your bank account since you last checked. Customers might have paid you and in all probability some direct debits will have come out for monthly commitments for items such as software. You might have paid for a few things on your business card, too, and all of these transactions need to be recorded in your accounting software.

Your accounting software should recognise any incoming receipts from customers as payments against 'invoices outstanding'. If you've raised lots of invoices for the same amount, your software will have a guess at which invoice the receipt relates to, but you should check that it matches the right invoice before clicking 'match' (or whatever terminology your software is using to record the invoice as paid).

You should have set up any supplier invoices you've received as 'invoices payable'. If payments have been made against those invoices and you can see money going out of the bank account in the bank feed, it should be a case of simply clicking 'match'. If the transaction was paid for at point of sale and a receipt was issued or if there is a supplier invoice but it hasn't already been set up in your accounting system, you will need to find the paperwork now and record it against the bank transaction. In our experience this is often the bit which takes the most time and big business owners are likely to procrastinate because finding paperwork for a number of different transactions (perhaps all from different suppliers) can be a bit of a hassle. The best way to speed up this process is to get into good habits early. This means taking photos of receipts and paperwork as soon as you receive them, ideally through an app, such as ReceiptBank, because as well as storing the photo, this will save you time with the data entry when you record that transaction.

Once you've recorded all of your transactions, you should check that the bank balance recorded in your accounting system agrees with your bank statement to make sure nothing is missing or has been duplicated in your accounts. Whether you still get paper bank statements or an email each month when your bank statement is ready to view, use this as the trigger to complete this task.

Some accounting software calculates what it thinks is your bank balance by taking whatever the last verified balance was and adding or subtracting the value of the transactions recorded in the bank feed. If they've all been recorded, the closing balance should agree with your physical bank statement, but if a transaction has been missed—very occasionally this happens with accounting software—or if a duplicate transaction has been made—this is less likely—the figures might not match and this is why we double-check. Most accounting software packages have a bank reconciliation function which you can use to complete this task quite easily and it will walk you through what you need to do if there are discrepancies. It's an important task to do because if your bank balance is out, you likely have an incorrect transaction somewhere meaning your profits are either over or understated.

Make adjustments

Depending on your business's speciality and set-up, there may be adjustments that you need to make to your accounting system, and these should be in your checklist.

If you have employees, you will need to run your weekly or monthly payroll, depending on how your staff are paid, and potentially post these transactions into your software. There's more information about posting payroll transactions in Chapter 6.

The other adjustment you'll need to make, if you're running a product-based business, relates to stock. Stock is recorded as a cost of sale when it's purchased, but each time you perform a stock-take you should post a journal to reflect the stock which is still in hand. This means that at any time you'll have an accurate picture of your business's costs and therefore profits, as well as the value of your stock.

Check you've been paid

The next thing you should do is to review your aged receivables. Running an aged receivables report will show you how much is due from each of your customers and how old the debt is. Like the aged payables report, the aged receivables report is generated as a table. It shows customers down one side and periods along the top to indicate how old each debt is. You'll see Current Receivables—invoices which aren't due for payment yet—and then other balances broken into columns to indicate how overdue they are.

I'd suggest running the most detailed report your accounting software can offer as this will arm you with all the information you need at a glance should you need to get on the phone to any of your customers. It will tell you invoice numbers, invoice dates, due dates and balances as well as how overdue each invoice happens to be.

How to chase customers for late payment

Raising invoices to your customers is one thing but getting them to actually pay you is something entirely different. If your customer hasn't paid you, it can feel daunting to chase them up. Don't be afraid to do it, though. When you went into business with them, you agreed to provide goods or services in exchange for payment and the terms and conditions of your contract will clearly state when the payment is due.

✓ Send a reminder

The first thing to do is to send a chaser from your accounting software. People are busy and there's a chance they may have missed your invoice or simply forgotten to make the payment, so a reminder might be enough to get the payment in. Most software will even send automated reminders for you.

✓ Send an email

If the reminder doesn't work, send a personal email to your customer. Receiving an automated reminder isn't particularly personal so use this email as an opportunity to check that they were happy with the goods or service (although hopefully you've already done this) and to ask them whether they received your invoice, to inform them that it's overdue and to ask when you can expect to receive payment. It's helpful to attach the invoice to your email in case they've lost it. If your customer is a business, it might be that the person you've been dealing with isn't the right person to deal with the invoice and they have a finance person or team who need to be copied in. In your email you can ask whether there's somebody else you should be dealing with (although don't let them use this as an opportunity to delay your invoice payment further).

✓ Get on the phone

The next step is to give them a call. You can do this straight after you've sent the email, or you might choose to skip the email altogether and get straight on the phone. I find that speaking to people on the phone is the most effective way to get in late payments because it reminds your customers that you're a real person. If you can have a nice chat with them, they're more likely to want to settle up.

I'd suggest trying to agree an actual payment deadline with the customer at this stage, and summing up at the end of the conversation with 'okay, so I look forward to receiving your payment this week' as this gives you an even better chance of securing payment. You'll need to follow up with an email so that you have a record of what was said. It also means that if you have to chase up the payment again, you can quote them on exactly what was said as you'll both have it in writing.

▶ Consider formal debt recovery

If your invoice remains overdue, you will need to start formal proceedings. The first step is to send a letter known as a 'letter before action' which states that if payment is not received within seven days, court proceedings will be started to recover the debt. If your client is another business, you can send a debt recovery letter instead, in which you can claim compensation for late payment and reasonable debt recovery costs as well as statutory interest on the overdue balance.

You can write this letter yourself or you can use a legal professional to help you and there are specialist firms who do just this. In our experience, clients get very upset when they receive a debt recovery letter so it must be handled well. However, it is usually a very effective way of recovering debt quickly and bringing the matter to an end, and if you have a client who doesn't pay, are they really the kind of client you want to retain anyway?

If the debt remains unpaid, the next step is to make a claim through the county court. Again, it is possible to do this yourself or you may choose to instruct a solicitor to do it on your behalf. Once the claim has been served against the debtor, they have 14 days to defend the claim, settle up or negotiate with you. After this a County Court Judgement (CCJ) can be made and enforcement action can be started, which ultimately means that a bailiff or enforcement officer could be dispatched to recover the debt in cash or in goods.

Summary

Through my bookkeeping practice, But the Books, I've worked with many small businesses who have fallen behind with their bookkeeping and, once we've helped them get back on track, they want to get back into good habits. When you let a backlog of work build up, it can feel daunting and overwhelming but doing it little and often will give you a much better chance of staying on top of things. Do two things: make time for bookkeeping by booking a non-negotiable appointment in the diary, and have a checklist which you work your way through each time.

You'll need to spend regular time on invoicing and chasing your customers, recording and paying supplier invoices and dealing with other transactions in your bank account for which you need to find the paperwork. If you're an employer, a VAT registered business or you sell products, you may also need to spend time recording your payroll, submitting your VAT return or recording stock movements, with some of these tasks coming up monthly and others quarterly.

Once you've established a routine and have been through your bookkeeping checklist a few times, the tasks you need to do should become second nature. That way, you can minimise your chance of returning to a position where you haven't done your bookkeeping for months.

CHAPTER 8
WHAT YOUR BOOKS CAN TELL YOU
ABOUT YOUR BUSINESS

So, you have a grasp of accounting basics, you've cleared your bookkeeping backlog, you're following your new checklist every week, and things are going well. Surely that's it now?

From a basics point of view, yes, it is. You're doing what you need to do, and you'll be in a good position to do your year-end filings. But I'm about to show you how good, up-to-date bookkeeping can offer so much more than just tax compliance: you can use it to gain a better understanding of your business. Believe me when I tell you that this is the fun bit (even if you really hate numbers).

Your accounts will provide insights which were simply impossible to reach before and you'll be able to put solid figures against the inklings you've had so far about your business's performance. Being knowledgeable about your business's finances will help you make better, informed decisions and you'll be ready to face questions, challenges and opportunities when they arise.

So, what can your numbers tell you?

Having read Chapter 6, you know all about the financial reports you need to produce for your business: the Profit and Loss (P&L) report and Balance Sheet needed for your company accounts and the profit figures you need for your year-end tax return.

These reports are great but they have one major limitation: it's likely that you produce them purely to tick boxes for HMRC and Companies House and we refer to this kind of reporting as 'compliance'. They are backwards-looking reports which are prepared to meet accounting rules and regulations rather than your specific needs as a business owner. With nine months to submit your tax return(s), there's little urgency to prepare them, and by the time you have them in front of you, so much time has passed that they're out of date, not reflective of the current situation in your business and practically useless for making decisions about the future.

To make these you're likely to want to have answers to questions you just won't see on the face of your Profit and Loss report and Balance Sheet for the last financial year.

But the good news is that by running the right reports at the right time you can use your accounts to answer questions like these:

- » *How much profit did I make from selling my products or services last month?*

- » *Is that better or worse than usual?*

- » *Should I stock more black T-shirts or white T-shirts?*

- » *How long do my customers take to pay me?*

- » *Will I have enough money to pay my VAT bill this quarter?*

- » *Can I afford to take on a bigger office space?*

- » *How much would I need to be turning over to pay for an extra member of staff?*

- » *If I'm making a decent profit, why is there no money in my bank account?*

Finance is an important part of any business's strategy and a good bookkeeper or accountant will not only make sure your bookkeeping is done well and that your accounts are up to date, but they'll also be able to support you in answering questions like these. They'll do this by helping you set forecasts and KPIs so that you can keep track of the figures you really need. We refer to this kind of reporting as 'management reporting' or 'management accounting'.

The beauty of management reporting is that it is not driven by accounting rules; its purpose is to provide information to answer management questions. It is not restricted to financial year ends and can be prepared for whichever period you want to monitor. It can also be segmented if you wish to monitor just specific products or services (provided that your bookkeeping has been done in a way which will allow you to see this differentiation).

As well as answering your questions, management reporting can also alert you to problems way before you might have known otherwise. How disadvantageous would it be for your business if you were unaware that you were facing a cash flow shortage for the coming quarter until your accountant prepared your year-end accounts? Exactly.

So, how can reports help you monitor the financial performance of your business? Let's start by looking at the main business reports (with which you're now familiar): the P&L report (aka income statement) and the Balance Sheet.

Profit & Loss (P&L) report

The P&L report looks over figures relating to past transactions, listing the value of your sales and expenditure and the profit you've made. Usually, this report is run for a full financial year at the year end, but there's no reason why you can't run one which covers a specific period of interest, whether that's the year to date or this week.

You'll find the P&L report useful if you want to see the trend in your sales figures, understand your costs or analyse your business's profit.

► Sales

If you're already tracking any figure in your business, it's likely to be sales. If you're not, then it's time to start, as it's a fundamentally important figure to keep an eye on.

Depending on what you sell and how your accounting system has been set up, your accounts will show the sales breakdown in varying levels of detail. You may just have one 'sales' figure, but you may also be able to break this down by product, region, country or some other category of your choice.

Monitoring your sales means that you'll be able to answer questions like:

» *Which is my best-selling product?*

» *Was I more profitable this month or last?*

» *Have I hit my sales target?*

» *In which month do I sell the most?*

» *When would be a good month to run a promotion?*

» *Did that advertising spend on white T-shirts result in more sales?*

► Profit

There are also two profit figures you'll see on the P&L report: gross profit and net profit, which are calculated like this:

Gross profit = Sales – cost of sales

Net profit = Sales – (cost of sales + overheads)

Gross profit tells you how profitable your products are and net profit shows you overall, after all other costs, how profitable the business is. These two figures are really important, and I often tell clients that if they're going to start monitoring any figures in their business, gross and net profit margins are a great place to start.

✓ Gross profit

Gross profit is essential. It tells you whether the goods or services you're selling are profitable. This is before you consider any overheads; it's simply the amount you're selling the item for minus any costs of producing or providing it. Let's say you source T-shirts, print them with your designs and sell them. Gross profit would be calculated by deducting the costs of making the T-shirt—the price you originally paid for the T-shirt and the printing cost—from the amount you receive from selling it.

Knowing your gross profit at this point tells you something. If you don't make a profit at this point, there's no way that you'll be able to cover your overheads, so it's critical to know how much gross profit you're making.

You can work out your gross profit as a whole on all the goods or services you sell in your business or on a product-by-product basis. The latter can be useful if you sell a variety of things as it'll allow you to compare and contrast, consider which are your most profitable lines and adjust prices of other goods and services accordingly.

Gross profit will help you answer questions such as:

» *What is my most profitable product or service?*

» *Are the costs associated with making white T-shirts higher this year than last year?*

» *Which products or services should I spend the most effort to sell so as to maximise my business's profits?*

✓ Net profit

Knowing your *net profit* is also vital as it tells you whether your business is covering its overheads. Failing to do so could mean that perhaps not enough gross profit is being made or your business's overheads are too high. Knowing your net profit figures, you can investigate these further. To remind you, your overheads are the general costs involved in running a business: rent, administrative staff salaries, subscriptions, legal and accountancy fees, website costs, and so on.

Overheads cannot be allocated to a specific product or service because they apply to your business as a whole, so it's not possible to view your net profit on a product-by-product basis.

Net profit will help you answer questions like:

» *How efficiently is my business turning sales into profit?*

» *Are my profits growing or declining over time? Why?*

» *Are profits falling over time because the business has become more expensive to run? If so, for what reason(s)?*

» *Am I incurring unnecessary costs? Am I employing too many staff members?*

» *Or are my sales prices simply too low?*

Your income, costs and profits are one side of the story when it comes to your business, but to get the whole picture we should also spend some time looking at your Balance Sheet.

Balance Sheet

As discussed in Chapter 6, your Balance Sheet gives you a snapshot of your business's financial position on one specific day, showing what the business owns and what it owes. Like the P&L report, it's usually run at the year end, but you can use it to give you a full view of your business at any time.

In terms of running a business from day to day, the three most important figures to keep an eye on are your bank balance, the amount your customers owe you, and the amount you owe your suppliers and other creditors.

► **Your bank balance**

Over the years, I've met several business owners who simply don't want to know about their books. Maybe you're one of them or maybe this describes you in the past. They keep an eye on their bank balance—some monthly, others daily—and if there's money in the bank then they assume that all is well. And maybe all is well, but your bank balance on one particular day doesn't tell you the full story.

It is very important to add monitoring your bank balance to your bookkeeping routine. Knowing that you have money in the bank is reassuring; knowing that you're about to run out means that you can take action.

Beware. Your bank balance doesn't take account of your next VAT bill or wage bill, nor whether customers are paying you on time. It doesn't take account of whether you're up to date with paying your suppliers, whether you're going to have to place a big order of stock next week or whether you're about to see a huge seasonal slump in sales if you're selling something of a seasonal nature (ice cream or big woolly jumpers, for example). It's vital that you check your bank balance alongside several other important pieces of data to see the whole picture.

If you've ever wondered how much cash you actually need, a good place to start is to ensure that you can cover your costs for the next three months. If things were going badly, this three-month buffer would give you the breathing space to take action whilst continuing to run your business if that were the right thing to do.

▶ **Debtors**

A customer who owes you money is known as a debtor or a receivable and if you invoice your clients or extend any type of credit to them, it's crucial to know whether they're paying you in full and on time. If they're not paying you, it's bad for your bank balance, and if you're not aware that they're not paying you, you could continue to sell to them despite their outstanding debts.

Looking at your Balance Sheet will tell you how much your debtors owe you at any one time; however, running an aged receivables report will tell you far more. If you need a reminder, head back to Chapter 7. Every time you review your aged receivables report, there are some things to look out for: firstly, which customers owe you money and how old their debts are;

secondly, how long your average customer is taking to settle their bill. This information will be hugely insightful, as it tells you how effective you are at chasing invoice payments and it will help you forecast your cash flow (more on this in Chapter 9).

▶ **Creditors**

As well as money owed to you, you also need to know about money you owe to others (known as your creditors or payables). Again, if you look at the creditors on your Balance Sheet, you'll see only one figure, but running an aged payables report will help you understand who you need to pay and when, which is more important for helping you forecast your cash flow. In this age when nearly everything is paid by direct debit or by card online, I sometimes think the aged payables report might become extinct, but if you're paying for anything off invoices, it's something you need to review.

When you should run reports

The P&L report and Balance Sheet give you a good overview of what's happening in your business. They're both essential year-end reports but we recommend that our clients review theirs quarterly, if not monthly, in order to keep a view of what's happening. You could even run them weekly if you wanted to. If you're using a good accounting system, you'll have the option to customise those reports in various ways such as splitting your sales into different categories or sectors (depending on which information you're entering into your software). This makes far more meaningful reports than those you run to tick boxes at the year end.

Answering questions about your business

You've got all of this great information, you're running some reports, and you even know what they mean.

How can you use all of this to really make sense of your business?

Well, it really depends on what you need to know so let's go back to those questions you might have about your business finances and address how you can use your accounts to answer them.

> » *How much profit did I make from selling my products or services last month?*
>
> You'll now know that to find out your profit, you need to use your P&L report. In order to answer this question, you'll need to run the report for last month and look at your gross profit figure. Depending on how you've recorded transactions in your accounting system—specifically whether you've used categories to analyse different products and services—you may be able to break down your sales, cost of sales and gross profit figures by product or service type. This will give you an even better idea of which areas of your business have been the most profitable.

> » *Is that better or worse than usual?*
>
> If you want to compare last month's performance to other months—and in this instance we're taking gross profit as a measure of success—you can compare the figures in your P&L report to those of previous months. Your accounting system should let you add comparative periods to your report; for example, you can compare last month's profits to the previous month, a series of previous months or to the same time last year. All of these allow you to gauge where this month sits in comparison to previous months.

> » *Do I make more money by selling product 1 or product 2?*
>
> If you're using categories to distinguish between different products when recording your income and expenditure, you'll be able to run a P&L report which breaks down sales costs and profits by product type. This lets you see the amount you're generating from the sales of each product and the associated cost and gross profit. If you're interested in which product generates the most sales income, which

generates the highest gross profit or which has the highest gross profit margin (not always the product you're selling the highest volume of), the information will be there in your P&L report.

» *How long do my customers take to pay me?*

You might have a feel for how long customers are taking to pay you, and an aged receivables report is a great place to start to find out precisely which invoices are overdue and which customers you need to be chasing up. However, this question can be answered by calculating a simple ratio, all made possible by having your accounts up to date and being able to run a P&L report and Balance Sheet. This ratio will give you the average number of days your customer is taking to settle your invoices and can be eye-opening in terms of understanding the effectiveness of your credit control processes.

We call this ratio 'debtor days' and to calculate it you need two pieces of information. Firstly, your average daily sales figure. You can calculate this by looking at your business's sales for the last 12 months (by running a P&L report) and dividing them by 365. This tells you on average how much you're invoicing each day. Secondly, you also need to know your debtors outstanding within the current timeframe. This figure is the 'trade receivables' or 'trade debtors' figure in your cost of sales.

The ratio is calculated as debtors divided by average daily sales, giving you a number in days which indicates how long it takes for your average customer to pay you.

Debtor days = Debtors / Average daily sales

» *Will I have enough money to pay my VAT bill this quarter?*

There are two pieces of information you'll need in order to answer this question: how much your VAT bill will be this quarter and how much money you'll have in the bank on the date it's due. Most accounting systems have a VAT feature which will allow you to view your growing VAT bill as you progress through the quarter and to finalise and submit the return at the quarter's end.

In fact, if you are VAT registered, almost certainly you should be submitting your return online via your software anyway. Knowing your VAT bill is the first part of the puzzle and you can use the VAT function of your accounting system to see where you are right now and estimate the quarter's total based on what you think will happen in the rest of the quarter. Alternatively, you might choose to look at last quarter's VAT bill for an estimate if your activity tends to be the same from quarter to quarter.

Knowing whether you'll have enough money to cover that bill requires you to forecast your cash flow, which is something we'll talk about in Chapter 9.

» *Can I afford to take on a bigger office space?*

A few years ago, we took on a client who had moved offices without anticipating all of the additional costs and the hit his bank balance was about to take. Knowing your numbers well will allow you to make a proper assessment of your business's financial situation before you sign on the line.

First things first: you need to consider all the costs. Most commercial rents are paid quarterly (although some are monthly), so find out how much you'll need to pay and when. Figures are often quoted without VAT so be sure of exactly what you'll be paying; if you're not VAT registered, you'll need to budget for an additional 20% on top of your rent. Also, find out whether there's a service charge or any other costs such as cleaning or room hire if you need meeting rooms.

Other costs which often get forgotten are the costs of legal support to help you with the tenancy contract, costs of moving offices, costs of IT, and new phone lines, all of which eat into your profit. Then there are the costs of furniture and equipment for the new office which will impact your cash flow, not to mention the likelihood that the landlord will want a hefty deposit and several months' rent up front. These costs all add up and should form part of the decision you make.

Whether you can afford it or not comes down to how much profit you're making (and whether there's capacity for increased cost), how much cash you have in the bank and what the additional space will allow you to do. If you're making a decent net profit you might be able to bear the higher rental costs. You may need the space because you're expanding your team, and employing more people will—in theory—allow you to take on more work. But, you need to remember that this is a hypothetical assumption and you don't know for sure that the extra work will come in. Profit and cash flow are two different things and although you may be able to afford it on paper, much of the decision will come down to whether you have cash in the bank to pay your bills. We'll cover cash flow in Chapter 9.

» *How much would I need to be turning over to pay for an extra member of staff?*

There are so many factors to consider when answering a question like this. First of all, you need to understand the costs involved of taking on that member of staff. As well as the obvious salary cost, as an employer you're likely to have to pay a pension contribution and employers' National Insurance contributions, as well as covering costs of recruitment, equipment, IT and training.

The turnover needed to cover these things depends on the costs involved, and it might help you to have a target for the amount of turnover each member of staff should generate, whether they're involved in sales or not. Of course, this figure depends on your margins, but in the creative industry—the industry we work with the most—business owners expect to see a return in terms of turnover of 4-10 times the salary for each employee. This is a large range and it does vary from business to business, but let's say you're a small business with low overheads. If you take on somebody with a salary of £20k, targeting £80k as your minimum additional turnover expectation gives you a number to aim for, and your understanding of potential additional work will help you to decide whether taking on that extra person is a viable option.

» *If I'm making a decent profit, why is there no money in my bank account?*

Contrary to popular belief, it is possible to be profitable but short of cash. There are many reasons why this might be and your accounts are the key to understanding what's going on.

The two most likely reasons why you're struggling for cash are that your receivables are not paying you on time or you've made a large investment in assets.

If you're running a business which invoices its clients, sales do not necessarily mean cash in the bank. You can raise an invoice but whether your client actually pays you is an entirely different matter. A good place to start if faced with this question is an aged receivables report. This will show you which invoices are overdue and by how long, and how much is outstanding. You can also calculate your debtor days ratio to understand how long your average customer is taking to pay you. These two sets of figures will be sure to help you understand whether debtors are the cause of your cash flow shortage.

Alternatively, you may have recently invested a significant amount in assets – equipment and machinery, for example. As explained in Chapter 6, assets are not an expense of the business so they don't affect your profit. As items which will be kept for a long time, they're recorded instead on your Balance Sheet. If you run a Balance Sheet now and one for your last year end or a year ago, you'll be able to see how your assets have changed. If they've increased significantly, it might be that your heavy investment in this area has led to a big cash outflow without any impact on profit.

Most accounting systems will allow you to run a cash flow report. This is a simple, backwards-looking report for any specific period which shows how much cash has come into the business and where it's come from, and how much cash has gone out and why. Other large outflows we see regularly are drawings (for our sole trader clients) and directors' loans or dividends (for our limited company clients). Taking money out of the business impacts your business bank balance so should be carefully thought about.

Summary

If you were running a business with a bag of receipts up until Chapter 5, think back. Is there any way you could have answered questions like this before you had your bookkeeping up to date and properly recorded? Isn't it wonderful what you can do now?

In this chapter we've looked at the reports you can run for your business. We've thought about what the P&L report and Balance Sheet can tell you and we've seen how they can answer questions you might have about your business.

There's so much more to share on this topic and so many more questions I can help you answer, but these questions are the ones I'm asked a lot. You may not be worried about your VAT bill or even be registered for VAT, but you might be worried about paying payroll in the next few months or whether you'll have next quarter's rent. Because accounts look backwards, they fail to tell you about the future of your business, so there are plenty of questions about your business and its future performance which you won't be able to answer using just your accounts. In the next chapter, we're going to look at budgets and forecasts and how these can help you understand your business even more.

CHAPTER 9
BUDGETING AND CASH FLOW FORECASTING

I recently attended a workshop on the other side of Bristol – somewhere I hadn't been before. If I'd just set off in the car, I could have easily missed a turning which would have resulted in a two-hour detour because of an unexpected road closure. But I didn't just get in the car and drive. I looked up the address of the venue on Google Maps, I checked where I could park, I scanned the traffic updates just before I left, and I used the satnav to make sure I stayed on course. I expect that's what you'd have done too.

But do you take the same approach to your business? Most small business owners know what their products and services are, they know who they're selling to, they even know how many times a week they want to be posting on social media, but finances can be an afterthought. I think this is because small businesses don't always have a clear strategy and many businesses start as side hustles which don't always need to be profitable from day one. Business owners often don't set goals for their businesses, certainly in respect of money, and without that real focus on what is and isn't working financially, it's easy to wake up one day and realise that your business is facing a cash flow crisis.

Business owners ask us all the time how they can make more money and where they should be cutting costs, and I tell them that if they set goals (or budgets) for income and expenditure and they stick to them, they'll soon have the information they need to answer those questions themselves.

Understanding your finances is key to working towards your business goals and budgeting puts you in control. In this chapter I'll tell you about the repercussions of failing to budget, how to set a budget, the difference between a budget and a cash flow forecast, and how software can help you set and monitor them.

The problem with not budgeting

Most of us have some kind of household budget and we know how much our bills come to each month. Sometimes we have to tighten our belts because there's something big to save for. Sometimes we spend a bit more than we should. Sometimes we can't resist an impulse buy. And this leaves us a bit short at the end of the month. Even though those numbers might not be written down, knowing how much money you have coming in and going out—and how much you should or shouldn't be spending on takeaways each month—is a budget.

Imagine if you had absolutely no idea how much was going in and out of your bank account. When you see something you really want to buy, how can you know whether you can afford it and still cover your mortgage payment for that month? Budgeting for a business is much the same, and the problems with failing to budget in business are very similar to those we face when we fail to budget in our personal lives.

▶   **The risk of failing to cover your costs**

As a business owner, if you don't set a budget, you're left open to the risk of not expecting or (even worse) not being able to pay a crucial bill. Just like with your household spending, your business probably has a number of regular commitments: salaries, rent, insurance, phone bills, utilities, software costs, etc. If you fail to pay one of these, you could find yourself losing something essential for running your business – your staff or premises being crucial examples.

► **An inability to plan for the future**

Even if you're covering all of those things comfortably each month, what you'll be finding less comfortable without a budget is that you'll never really know exactly where your money is coming from or where it's going. This means that you might be investing your time and energy into activities which aren't profitable or important for the business, or you might be unable to take up certain opportunities—for example, taking on new premises or a member of staff—because of uncertainty about their impact on your business finances.

► **Difficulty in accessing funding**

You might be actively seeking investment or hoping to take up one of the many small business grants which are available. Having a short and long-term budget will be crucial in being able to secure that funding or even for you to work out whether you should consider applying in the first place. I recently found out about a grant available to support small businesses with coaching costs. Businesses were able to claim back £1,000 in grant funding providing they committed to spending £2,000 (although the claim couldn't be made retrospectively). This is a perfect example of a missable opportunity: if you hadn't taken the time to sit down and plan ahead, you wouldn't know how much money you wanted to commit to training in the future.

Why you should budget

Having a well thought-out budget will allow you to plan for other things based on your finances for the months and years ahead and give you something to monitor your business's performance against. It might seem boring but by monitoring how things are going every single month, you can review your business's profitability, confirm or question the assumptions you're making about everything from sales volumes to office costs, and think about how you spend your business's money.

Being armed with the story of where you are heading will put your business in good stead. It will help you make decisions which are in line with your financial goals. It will encourage you to avoid distractions which will detract from your goals. It will help you bring the business back on track quickly if spending goes astray. Times change and opportunities change and the great thing about budgeting is that your budget can be adapted to fit the circumstances. But you will still have a plan – a calculated route to follow which gives you the best chance of getting to where you want to go.

The difference between a budget and a cash flow forecast

A *budget* is a document which lists out how much income you expect to receive and how much expenditure you expect to incur based on what you know about your business for the coming period. Income and expenditure targets are allocated to each of the headings you expect to see in your Profit and Loss report and give you something to monitor your actual income and expenditure against. Budgets tend to be built for the twelve months ahead, usually for the next financial year.

A *cash flow forecast* is a document which shows how much cash you expect to have in the bank in the future based on your expectations for the business's performance. Cash flow forecasts can be built for the year ahead or longer but are most accurate for shorter periods such as quarters.

Client story – Rachel

Rachel runs a small design agency and started working with us because she wanted a better grasp on what was coming in and going out of the business. She wanted to be more profitable and having faced some cash shortages in the past, she needed to know how much money she'd have in the bank from month to month.

We worked with Rachel to build a budget which we could monitor monthly on her behalf. We started by asking how much money she expected the agency to earn each month and what she anticipated the costs to be.

Going through the process of setting a budget gave Rachel the insight she needed to change course and focus on her most profitable business activities. She was able to understand the profitability of her main sources of income and to make the decision to focus on pursuing sales of one service over another. As well as making her more money, this meant that she would have cash available to hire staff and scale up her business, which was something she hadn't felt confident enough to do previously because she just wasn't clear on the numbers.

Being profitable is one thing but having cash in the bank is quite different. Going through the process of setting a budget will give you the figures you need to understand both. A budget is a projection of your activity, your sales, and your expenses and what this means for profits. A cash flow forecast takes these figures and any other amounts going in and out and tells you what they mean for your business bank balance.

Some figures will show up in both your budget and your cash flow forecast, while others will show up in different ways. Let's take a simple example:

When Rachel invoices her customers, she gives them 30 days to pay. However, she knows that one of her biggest customers works by their own rules and, despite her best efforts, they usually take 60 days to pay. She has guaranteed monthly work from that customer (let's say for £1,000) and takes on extra project work from them roughly every three months (let's say the average project costs them £1,500).

If this were her only income, Rachel's budget would show £1,000 of income in both months 1 and 2 and £2,500 in the third month. But, when looking at her cash flow, the money will not come into Rachel's bank account in months 1, 2 and 3 because, if the client takes 60 days to pay, she probably won't be paid until months 3, 4 and 5.

Budget:

▷   Month 1 – £1,000

▷   Month 2 – £1,000

▷   Month 3 – £1,000 + £1,500 (project) = £2,500

Cash flow:

▷   Month 1 – £0

▷   Month 2 – £0

▷   Month 3 – £1,000 (month 1)

▷   Month 4 – £1,000 (month 2)

▷   Month 5 – £1,000 (month 3) + £1,500 (month 3's project) = £2,500

As you can see, a cash flow forecast is based on a budget but is different because of the effect of timing on the cash flows.

▶   **What about VAT?**

If you're VAT registered, the differences can become a bit more technical. Let's take this example a step further. But first keep in mind that if you're not VAT registered, you need to budget for VAT on your expenditure as it is a cost to you as a business; you're not able to claim it back so it does hit your profit.

If Rachel were VAT registered, she would charge her customer 20% VAT on top of her normal rate, and this would be reflected on her invoices. In her budget she should completely disregard the fact that VAT is being charged to her customers or that she's paying VAT on her purchases. This is because VAT has nothing to do with profit and a budget is purely based on income, expenditure and profit. Businesses simply collect VAT on behalf of HMRC and pay it across to them (usually quarterly).

Rachel's budget would still show income of £1,000 in months 1 and 2 and £2,500 in month 3. Her cash flow forecast would be quite different, though. Although the work costs £1,000, Rachel's customer would be paying £1,200 (as this includes VAT at 20%). The month in which she did some project work as well would equate to a receipt of £3,000. Keeping it really simple, this means that Rachel's cash flow forecast would show £1,200 coming in for both months 3 and 4 (remember: the client takes around 60 days to pay) and £3,000 in month 5. Let's say Rachel's on the standard VAT scheme and her VAT quarter ends in months 3, 6, 9 and 12 with VAT due to be paid to HMRC by the 7th of months 5, 8, 11 and 2 respectively. She will also need to forecast for £900 of VAT (£200 each for months 1 and 2, and £500 for month 3) to be paid to HMRC in month 5.

Cash flow:

▷   Month 1 – £0

▷   Month 2 – £0

▷   Month 3 – £1,000 (month 1) + £200 (VAT) = £1,200

▷   Month 4 – £1,000 (month 2) + £200 (VAT) = £1,200

▷   Month 5 – £1,000 (month 3) + £200 (VAT) + £1,500 (month 3's project) + £300 (VAT) -£900 (VAT liability) = £2,100

We've only looked at income here, but expenditure is approached in the same way. In your budget consider the amounts without any VAT and record them in the month you'll be billed. In your cash flow forecast you need to include the VAT you'll pay and record the spend in the month you'll actually settle up and make the payment; when paying for things by card or direct debit, this is likely to be the same date, but when invoiced for items, you won't necessarily settle up straight away.

Timing differences with VAT and other taxes can make building a cash flow forecast a bit more complicated than building a budget, but it can be done accurately with a bit of patience. I'd suggest using your budget as your starting point, working through each of your income and expenditure categories one at a time to make sure that things are included in the forecast for the right month. Then, think about whether there are other amounts going in and out of your account which you might not have picked up on; typical ones are VAT payments to HMRC if you're VAT registered, PAYE, National Insurance and pension deductions if you're an employer, and corporation tax or income tax depending on which legal form your business takes.

How to build a budget

When I trained as an accountant, there were various budget-building techniques we studied and practiced, but I'm going to talk you through one method which I think is really well suited to small businesses, particularly if you're building a budget for the first time. It's called zero-based budgeting and I like it because it makes you challenge the costs you're incurring. If you've been in business for a little while, you may not have thought about which of your costs are necessary for running your business. The idea in zero-based budgeting is that you make no assumptions about anything that's happened in the past; you look at each cost and income stream on its own merit, deciding what you really need to be spending on and what you really want your income streams to be. This gives you a fresh start. A budget can be set for any period, but traditionally they're set for a year at a time, covering one financial year.

▶ **Income**

Let's say you're a freelancer and you're not VAT registered. You charge for your time at £250 per day and you want to know that you are likely to have work for 15 days per month. Your budget for income would therefore be £3,750 per month. Now, a note on reality here. There's no point saying that you'll work 15 days per month if you know it's unlikely to happen, or that you're going to charge £250 per day if you know the going rate is only £200. This would make your budget frustratingly difficult to achieve.

If you know you're doing some training to upskill yourself—allowing you to charge a higher rate—or you know there's going to be a shortage of people with the skills you have—meaning that you're likely to get 5 extra days' work in July—then by all means, use those assumptions in your calculations when setting your budget. If you're doing a big marketing drive in three months' time and you are confident that it will increase the number of days you're able to work, then make an assumption and build it into your budget, too. Your income budget will become your sales target, giving you a focus each month to ensure that you're selling and invoicing the right amount, and helping you to ask the right questions if not.

► **Expenditure**

Expenditure is a really interesting part of building a budget because it allows you to completely rethink everything you know about how your business works. Taking control of your expenses can also work wonders for your profitability and it's fascinating to see business owners delve into what they're spending and decide whether they are using their funds wisely. When building your budget for costs and starting from a zero base, you need to go back to basics and think about what you need to spend money on as if you were starting from scratch.

Firstly, think about what you're selling. If it's a product, how is it made? What are the components and where do you source them? How is it packaged and delivered to customers? What's the best delivery option to suit your needs? Is there a cheaper supplier to work with or one which offers better value?

If you sell a service, what are the costs of making that happen? Who's involved in delivering it? How much does their time cost? Is the way you're delivering things now the way you'll deliver things in the future? Will you move online? How will that change your costs?

Then, you need to look at your overheads: your staff, office costs, software, travel, professional fees, etc. To meet your intended sales target, which of these are really necessary?

Let me tell you a bit about building But the Books because we've been on this journey, too. I started the business as a one-woman band; But the Books was my freelance side hustle. In order to scale up, though, I needed a team and we needed IT equipment, phones and desks. A good way to think about staffing is to think about how many work-hours you need to get things done. This was certainly the case for us, and by knowing those numbers and being able to place a salary on the level of skill and number of hours we needed, it was possible to build a picture of our ideal team and assign costs to it for our budget. The costs of pensions and National Insurance, training, software licences and desk space also needed to be considered, but once I knew how many people I was building a budget around, the rest fell into place.

There are plenty of other things which aren't dependent on your headcount, though, like your website, marketing, and insurance. You might choose to look at what you've spent in the past to remind you of the types and amounts of costs you incur. However, always challenge decisions you've made already, like whether your supplier offers the best value for money.

Setting a budget isn't complex, but you do need to take some time out to sit down, think about your plans for the coming year and estimate the associated income and costs. It's a great opportunity to question assumptions you've made in the past and the result is a valuable document you can use to benchmark against to keep you on course.

How to build your cash flow forecast

Your budget is a really good starting point for your forecast. Just like with your budget, the first thing to do is to choose the period for forecasting. It makes sense for your annual forecast to tie in with the dates of your budget. However, the forecast will be most accurate for the coming month or quarter simply because its accuracy relies on how closely your actual income and expenditure match your budget and, I hate to say it, but there's no way your budget will be spot on.

Forecasting your cash position further out can be less reliable, as income and expenditure drifts from the budget, but you can monitor and change your forecast at any time. The main thing is to get started. I suggest that you lay out your forecast as a table, with income and expenditure categories down the side and months (or weeks if you prefer) along the top.

The next step is to estimate what your starting bank balance will be at the time when your forecast begins. If you're starting your forecast from today, then simply check your bank account. If your forecast begins a month or two in advance, you're going to need to do a bit more estimating to work out where you'll be at that point. Don't forget to take into account all of the bank accounts you have. As well as your business's current account, you might have savings accounts or foreign currency accounts. Some of our clients also have money tied up in their Paypal accounts so make sure you note all of these balances down.

The next step is to look at income on your budget to tell you how much will be coming in and at what time. As well as sales income, take account of any other sources of income. Have you agreed to sell some equipment? Are you expecting to receive a grant or a cash inflow from an investor? Both will impact your bank balance.

Then, look at what's going out. Your budget will tell you what your expected costs are. Think about the timing so that you can allocate them against the relevant month, as some things can be paid off invoice with perhaps 30-day terms, whereas other costs will be paid straight away by card or direct debit. Think about your regular costs: your salaries bill, rent, utilities, software and materials costs. Don't forget tax payments like your VAT bill if you're VAT registered or your corporation tax bill if you're running a limited company.

If you have only a few incomings and outgoings, you might be able to just list out your commitments. It really is as simple as opening balance + money in – money out = closing balance. For more complicated businesses, a table with columns for each month will be a better way to lay things out. You might choose to use software which has been built specifically for this purpose, which is something we'll look at in the next section.

A word on software

We've looked at how to build a budget and a cash flow forecast but we haven't really considered which tool you'll use to do it. At But the Books we work with a number of businesses on budgeting and forecasting and we know that tables of numbers can be pretty visually unappealing. It's true that a spreadsheet is a good way to store the data you need, and that some accounting software has the built-in ability to budget and monitor performance, but we know from experience that graphs and visuals are so much better for helping business owners understand how things are looking for their business.

Because of this, we build our forecasts using specialised forecasting software, meaning that we can share beautiful graphs and visuals with our clients. These help them understand what's going to cause spikes or dips in cash flow and when and to help them plan ahead. There is some great software out there. You might want to google Futrli, Float and Fluidly to name just three or you might choose to work with a bookkeeper or accountant to help you make the most of this powerful software.

How to monitor a budget or cash flow forecast

Once you've built your forecast, you should monitor it regularly to find out whether you're on track and, if you're not—or if something's changed in the business which will affect your budgeted figures—then revise it.

I suggest that business owners review their actual figures against their budgets every month and this can be done in a simple spreadsheet where you have a column for your budgeted figures for the month, a column for your actual figures and a column for your variances (your actual minus your budget). You might also decide to have a separate set of columns which looks at budgets, actuals and variances for the year to date as this can give a more detailed picture of how the business is performing than just the previous month's figures. Your job, then, is to go through each row (each line representing a different type of income or expenditure) and challenge why there's a variance between the budget and the actual (if there is one). It takes patience and a lot of digging but by looking at these variances you'll start to understand where things might not be going to plan and then you can take action.

How to improve your cash flow

If you've been thinking about building a cash flow forecast—or maybe even started already—you might have some questions about how you would go about improving your cash flow if you were facing a challenging time. For this reason, I thought I'd end the chapter by sharing a popular blog post from our website. We often work with start-ups and I can't tell you how many times they've asked me how they can improve their cash flow. It's a common problem and the principles are the same, whether you're making sales of £5,000 or £5m.

So, here are six top ways to improve your cashflow:

▶ **Make sure that customers pay you**

It sounds obvious, but if you don't chase your late payers, you're missing out on money. If you're using a good accounting system, it will be easy to run an aged receivables report. This is a list of your customers, values of outstanding invoices, and ages of each invoice. Armed with this report, start by focusing on your largest and oldest overdue invoices to get that money rolling in.

▶ **Change your payment terms**

Many businesses send invoices giving customers 30 days to pay, but you might want to think about reducing those terms to 14 days or payment due on receipt of goods. If you're selling a service, you might even consider asking customers to pay you partially or wholly in advance or offering a discount if they pay for a year in advance rather than paying monthly.

▶ **Use direct debit**

Why not ask regular customers to pay you by direct debit? Knowing the money will be collected from your customer's bank account on an agreed date is so much more convenient for you than having to chase up people who forget to pay their invoices.

▶ **Know your big payments**

Make sure you know the dates of your regular large payments and write them in your diary or, even better, set them up as recurring bills in your accounting system. Find out how much you usually pay and set some money aside every month to make sure that you have the money ready to pay your bills when they're due.

▶ **Budget for the smaller stuff**

It's easy to spend, spend, spend when you know that you can get whatever you want delivered the next day using a one-click payment. These small purchases quickly add up, though. Sit down and think about what the business really needs in the next quarter or year and set yourself a budget. Then, monitor what you've spent against that budget every month.

▶ **Pay your suppliers as late as possible**

When you receive invoices from your suppliers, look at the payment terms and schedule those payments to be made as close to (but not later than) the due date as possible. If you're using an accounting system, you can do this by simply recording each bill as it's received and also recording its due date.

Summary

In this chapter we've looked in detail at why you need a budget and cash flow forecast for your business and how to build each of them. We've looked at how income and expenditure appear differently in a budget than in a cash flow forecast, how forecasting software might give you a more visual and user-friendly view of your business's numbers and how to monitor your actual figures against your budget and forecast.

You might feel inspired to go away and build a really detailed budget and cash flow forecast for the coming year. You might just plan out the next few months. Either way, once your forecast is in place, you can be confident about what's coming up, and I'm sure you'll agree that having this additional insight into your business gives you so much more control.

In the next chapter, we're going to take that insight even further and start setting key performance indicators (KPIs)—or, simply, targets—which can help you understand and monitor your business more easily.

CHAPTER 10
UNDERSTANDING YOUR BUSINESS BETTER

I wanted to call this chapter *'How to use KPIs to understand your business better'* but some time ago, I was talking to one of our clients, suggesting some KPIs to track in his business, and he stopped me: "What's a KPI?!" I'm pleased he asked because jargon in the business world is common but so unnecessary, and we often fall into the trap of using it. My client was really keen to measure his gross profit margin and his average sales value once I was clear about what I meant.

KPIs, what they are and why you need them

A KPI is a key performance indicator, a target or measure of performance which you can set and track to tell you how your business is performing and whether it's hitting its goals (you can also use them for people). Sales, customer satisfaction and financial performance are the areas of business which business owners really want to know more about. Once you start tracking your KPIs, you can measure your performance against a previous period or target, compare one part of your business to another, or compare your business to a competitor.

In this chapter I'm going to cover how KPIs can provide even more insight into how your business is doing. I'll tell you about some KPIs routinely tracked by our clients and others which you might find useful for your business.

I come from a corporate background where tracking key performance indicators was a big job we did every month. In fact, one of the organisations I worked for had a whole performance indicator reporting process to go through each quarter, with different members of staff tracking different KPIs not just related to finances but to every aspect of the services delivered by the organisation, and all of the things which went on behind the scenes. We measured everything from customer response times to number of employee sick days.

For a small business, a document tracking this much detail would, of course, be overkill. But I do feel that it's very important—particularly for small business owners—to track a handful of KPIs which give them real, concrete information about how their businesses are doing.

Knowing these stats and comparing them month on month will help you ask important questions about trends in your business and be armed with the facts you need to make decisions about your business's future.

Why you need KPIs

You've read this far so you'll know all about the financial reports you need to produce for your business—the P&L report and Balance Sheet you need for your company accounts and the profit figures you need for your year-end tax return(s)—but what do these reports really tell you about your business?

> » *How much profit did you make on each sale of product X last month and how did that compare to the previous month?*

> » *How long do your customers take to pay you?*

> » *How long does a visitor stay on your website?*

If you've ever had questions like these, you could benefit from setting some KPIs. Having a dashboard or a spreadsheet—or even a piece of paper—where you work out and monitor those vital bits of information each month will help you answer the questions that are important for you to understand how your business is doing.

KPIs you should be measuring

The things you will want to understand about your business will change based on your priorities. At our bookkeeping practice we recommend that business owners set some specific targets and KPIs based on the questions they have about their businesses and add to and develop them over time so that they remain relevant as the business grows and evolves. There are no KPIs which you must monitor; they could cover absolutely anything you want to understand about your business.

In order to understand your sales, you might be interested in sales volumes, average sale value, or repeat orders. If you were interested in the efficiency of your team, you might track headcount, average revenue per employee, or monthly sales for each member of your sales team (if you have one). Cash flow might be on your mind, in which case you could track how long your customers take to pay you (debtor days), how many days' worth of cash you have in the bank, or simply your bank balance. If you want to tighten up your expenditure, you might be looking at profit margins, comparing them across products or services. If the numbers are there, you can measure them.

You can also compare your financial results against non-financial figures in your business and this can give you some really interesting insights. Want to know your profit per square metre of office space? Want to know how much you spend on marketing per new customer? Now you can.

Obviously, not every KPI is going to be useful to you, and the number of options can be overwhelming. The best place to start is to 1) think about which questions you want answered and 2) choose the measures which answer those questions. The figures need to be useful to you otherwise you won't be interested in measuring them. You also need to have the data readily available or it will be a chore to work out and you'll lose motivation; you need to find a way to make your KPIs straightforward and manageable.

I'm talking about the kinds of things where you can just run a report out of your accounting system, divide one number by another and have the figure for the month. Be realistic. If you have to build a whole process which involves logging into several different systems and opening a multitude of spreadsheets, you're just not going to do it. Make things as simple as possible for yourself.

▶ Sales KPIs

✓ Monthly sales

I always suggest that business owners monitor their monthly sales. If you know the sales figures you need to hit each month in pounds, it's easy to translate this into a quantity of units you need to sell each month. This can be easier to deal with than a spreadsheet full of pound signs.

✓ Revenue per employee

If you have a team, this can be an incredibly useful KPI, as it helps you keep track of how much income is being earned per member of the team. Sales are divided by the number of full-time equivalent staff you have, regardless of their role, although in some sales-focussed businesses, it's common to measure revenue per salesperson. It will help you to determine whether your headcount is appropriate, identify where your team might be inefficient, and perhaps tell you whether you have enough income to justify hiring another person.

This KPI is calculated by dividing revenue by the number of employees, so if you make sales of £200,000 and you have four staff members, you earn £50,000 per employee. You may be able to benchmark against an industry average to gauge whether your KPI is what you should expect.

✓ Average sale value

This is a very useful KPI for measuring the average revenue received from every sale. It's particularly straightforward to calculate if you invoice your clients, as it's calculated by dividing revenue by the number of invoices raised.

If you sell in person, taking payments through your till, you might like to calculate revenue divided by number of sales transactions if your till will give you this information, or revenue earned each day the shop was open. Each of these will give you a meaningful measure of your sales revenue and help you identify opportunities to upsell to your customers, for example, by offering add-ons before they check out online or, in customer-facing environments, by identifying popular days to justify longer opening hours.

► Profit-related KPIs

I suggest that all businesses monitor their profit margins. They are business essentials and once you know your current profit margin and the profit margin you want to reach, you can take actions, like reviewing your cost base or raising your prices, which help you get closer to these goals.

✓ Gross profit margin

Gross profit is simply how much money (profit) is left over after you've paid the direct costs associated with producing the product or service. Gross profit margin is gross profit divided by revenue expressed as a percentage.

If you sell wedding cakes for £500 and your ingredients amount to £100, you make a £400 gross profit on each cake. This means that your gross profit margin is 80%.

If you're a graphic designer designing stationery for a client for which you'll charge £1,000, but the direct costs (including printing) are £400, you'll make a gross profit of £600 or 60%.

This is a useful KPI because it helps you keep track of whether your direct costs are eating into your profit margins for each product or service line. If you make a loss on a sale before you've started covering your overheads, you might want to reconsider the suppliers you're using for your direct costs or the sales price of your product or service.

✓ Net profit margin

Taking this one step further, net profit is how much money (profit) is left over after you've paid all your business costs expressed as a percentage.

If you make sales of £100,000, your direct costs are £20,000 and your overheads are a further £50,000, you will make a net profit of £30,000 or 30% (£30,000 divided by £100,000, multiplied by 100).

Net profit is generally calculated for the whole business and it's a useful KPI as it gives you an overview of how the business is doing.

✓ Break-even point

Break-even is important, especially if you are new in business and perhaps not profitable yet. The break-even point answers the question, "how much do I need to sell in order to cover my overheads?" This is important to know because all businesses have some overheads, whether this is the cost of rent, insurance, professional subscriptions, or maybe even staff.

To calculate your break-even point, simply add up all of the monthly overheads your business incurs in order to simply stand still. This is how much you need to sell each month to keep the business open.

▶ Cash flow-related KPIs

✓ Cash-to-debt ratio

If your business has debt—perhaps an overdraft or from some borrowing— you want to know whether you will have enough money in the bank to cover the debt repayments which will be coming up in the short term.

To calculate this KPI you need to know how much money you have in the bank and divide that by the debt repayments that you will need to make in the coming 12 months. For example: if you currently have a bank balance of £20,000 and you have £10,000 of repayments due in the next year, you will have a cash-to-debt ratio of 2, which more than covers your debt repayments. If you had a cash-to-debt ratio of less than 1, this would signal a potential cash flow problem within the next year.

✓ Debtor days

This is an important KPI to track if you invoice your customers. If your customers are slow at paying you, it can cause all sorts of cash flow problems and this KPI tells you at a glance how many days (on average) your customers are taking to pay you. In fact, this is one of my favourite KPIs because if you get it under control, it can make a huge difference to your cash flow.

It's calculated by taking the value of invoices currently outstanding, dividing it by the average value of sales invoiced for the year, and then multiplying this figure by 365. So, if you are currently waiting for £30,000 in outstanding invoices and, on average, you invoice around £200,000 per year, your average customer is taking 55 days to pay you.

If your payment terms are 30 days, this is a warning sign that your credit control function isn't very efficient and needs some attention. This might prompt you to do some credit control work or change the way customers can pay. Options here are encouraging customers to pay via direct debit or pay deposits in advance, or you can tighten up on whom you extend credit to.

► **Other KPIs**

✓ **Customer acquisition cost**

One grey area for many businesses is the value of their marketing spend. Marketing can cost a lot of money and if you're marketing in several places, it can be difficult to know which marketing campaign is paying off and which isn't.

One way to keep track of your customer acquisition cost is to record of all of your new leads, identifying how they found you. You can ask them in person or online when they place their orders. You can then categorise spend on different marketing campaigns so that you can divide the cost of a campaign by the number of leads generated by that specific campaign. This will tell you the average cost of each client acquired by each marketing campaign.

For example, imagine that in January you spent £2,000 on Facebook ads and £5,000 on a newspaper ad. You generated 100 new leads, 50 of which came from Facebook, 40 from the newspaper ad and 10 from referrals. Your customer acquisition cost from the Facebook campaign was £40 (the £2,000 spent on Facebook ads divided by the 50 customers who told you that they found you through Facebook) and £125 from the newspaper ad (the £5,000 spend divided by 40 new clients). The cost of acquiring the 10 new clients on referral was £0.

This might lead you to focus more spending on Facebook ads since, for you, they are more cost effective than newspaper ads. You might even consider trialling a referral programme with a cash incentive as this is also generating plenty of leads and, provided the incentive was less than £40, it would still be your cheapest method of marketing.

✓ **Non-financial customer KPIs**

Of course, there are plenty of non-financial KPIs you can measure. If you have an online community, you'll want to know how many members you have, and you might have a target for number of members and monthly growth of membership. Most businesses want to measure customer satisfaction, and this could be based on results of a survey post-sale or the review scores you get on an independent review site. If you sell a product, you might want to monitor your customer returns percentage. You might also want to track website visits, Instagram followers, or mentions in the press – the list really is endless and driven entirely by what's important to you and your business.

Where to track KPIs

Most clients like to have a monthly or quarterly dashboard which they can keep up to date and look at regularly. We provide a monthly report to our management-reporting clients, as well as a live dashboard linked to their accounting software which they can access via their login. But, you might not need this much detail and, if you don't, a simple spreadsheet might be enough.

The important thing is to make the information accessible so you can refer to it whenever you need it for decision-making because that's the point; this is not data for the sake of data.

If you make a monthly report for your finances, an obvious place to keep your KPIs is at the front or back of this document. Alternatively, you might like to keep them on a spreadsheet you refer to regularly, add them to a whiteboard you have in the office or jot them down on a quick reference sheet you always have on your desk.

Keeping your KPIs up to date requires a certain level of discipline, so I suggest that you add this exercise to your monthly finance process and pop it in the diary so that you remember to do it. There's nothing worse than missing it for a few months and then spending a whole afternoon processing the backlog, but if you stay on top of it, you'll quickly find that you build up a nice document of KPIs which will help you identify trends in your business and flag up when you need to take action.

How to decide on targets

It's important to set targets for each of your KPIs so that you know what you're measuring against. You might have a business plan or a strategy document which can help you with this. Alternatively, you might want to calculate your current KPIs and use your knowledge of your business to set goals for the future and then measure against them. Another option is to benchmark against other similar businesses. Some businesses publish information about particular performance measures, but you can also learn more by speaking to fellow business owners in your circle. I'm always surprised by how open other businesses are about the rates they charge, their growth rates and their profit margins. Similarly, business consultants or coaches come into contact with a lot of other businesses, so you'll find that they have an informed idea of industry averages.

Summary

At But the Books, our core business comprises of a monthly bookkeeping service, but we know that once you have the fundamentals in place, you can reap the benefits of your numbers. People sometimes resist setting and measuring KPIs because putting them together is time consuming and some people think it's just data for the sake of data.

Hopefully what I've shown you in this chapter is just how much insight you can gain into how your business is doing and where you can tighten up and improve just by tracking a handful of useful statistics. You don't even have to do it yourself; a good bookkeeper will be able to do this for you if you have neither the time nor the inclination, and we're going to talk about this in the next chapter.

CHAPTER 11
PAYING SOMEONE TO HELP YOU

There are two main reasons why clients come to us: either they don't have the time to do their own bookkeeping or they don't have the expertise. You've likely picked up this book and read this far because you've recently started your own business and you wanted a how-to guide which gives you the confidence to do your own bookkeeping. I hope you'll say that this book has helped you with that. But, just because you can do it yourself, it doesn't mean that you should, and when you get to the point when there aren't enough hours in the day to do everything and that you're being distracted from what you should really be doing (running your business), bookkeeping might be one of the first things you choose to outsource.

In this chapter I'll talk about the difference between a bookkeeper and an accountant, what a bookkeeper does and how they can help you, how to choose a good bookkeeper, and how to prepare for your first meeting.

Client story – Lisa

Lisa came to us for an accounting system setup, having always kept her records in a spreadsheet. She was over the VAT threshold, so she needed to start keeping digital records to comply with Making Tax Digital, which came into effect in 2019. Lisa is a very intelligent scientist; she told me that she had read our blog posts, she had done lots of research into which accounting system was best for her and had decided that she wanted to use Xero. She felt like she should be able to set up Xero herself but she couldn't bring herself to get started knowing that she'd have to work through her spreadsheet, check she'd recorded each receipt in her pile of receipts, connect her bank account and work through her transactions for the past 3 months. It wasn't a good use of her time, so she chose to outsource it to us.

What does a bookkeeper do?

People often tell me that they're not sure whether they need a bookkeeper and I think it's because many people don't actually know what a bookkeeper does. They know that their accountant's there to help them out with their year end, but what does a bookkeeper do?

Different bookkeepers offer different services which tend to include:

✓ **Sending invoices and credit control**

Bookkeepers can send invoices to your customers and tell you which customers have not yet paid. They can chase outstanding invoices and tell you whether they're having trouble getting specific customers to pay so that you can take action and decide whether to stop selling to these customers in the future.

✓ **Recording purchases**

When you receive invoices from your suppliers, your bookkeeper will record these into your financial system, making a record of the date the invoice is due for payment. They'll make sure you're aware of which invoices need paying by which date and, depending on the services you've agreed with your bookkeeper, they might pay these on your behalf from your bank account.

✓ Keeping your financial records up to date

Your bookkeeper will review your bank transactions, ensuring that other expenses are recorded correctly in your financial system and that you have proof with a receipt or other form of documentation.

✓ Payroll

If you have employees, your bookkeeper can arrange payroll, prepare payslips, arrange salary payments, and prepare the correct returns for HMRC.

✓ Help you understand your business finances

If you need to know how much you've paid a particular supplier this year, how much you're spending each month on train tickets or who's been your most lucrative customer, your bookkeeper can help you by preparing a report using your financial system.

✓ VAT returns

If you're VAT registered, your bookkeeper can make sure that you're keeping the right information about VAT paid and received and complete your VAT returns for you.

✓ Self-assessment

Bookkeepers can prepare self-assessment tax returns, they can ensure you're reporting the correct income and expenditure figures to HMRC and that you've claimed expenses the business is entitled to claim and that you haven't claimed anything you shouldn't.

As well as the specific technical work your bookkeeper can do, there is so much more to be gained from this relationship.

A good bookkeeper will give you support during the year

Your accountant's there to help you at the end of the year but they might not be helping you with your day-to-day finances. Your bookkeeper is a friendly finance person to help you keep on top of your business finances from day to day. Provided that they do a good job of your bookkeeping, it should save you money with your accountant at the end of the year.

✓ **They'll give you the information you really need about your business**

A good bookkeeper won't just record your transactions for you. They'll also show you how to use your accounting system to get the information you really need about your business. That might mean giving you training to help you get the best from your accounting system, or providing you with a monthly report which helps you understand your business's numbers better.

✓ **They'll help you improve your processes**

Small businesses often favour spreadsheets for keeping their accounting records, but updating these records can become complicated and time -consuming as a business grows. Small businesses often end up with lots of manual workarounds, which become cumbersome and confusing. A good bookkeeper can sort this out by helping you set up processes which are best practice and easy to follow.

✓ **They'll give you peace of mind**

By hiring a bookkeeper, you'll know that a financial professional is casting their eye over your figures. You'll know that transactions are being recorded correctly and that you are up to date. This will make everything easier for you at your year end, and will make sure that you have the right financial information to understand different things about your business throughout the year.

How to choose a good bookkeeper

A lot of my clients initially make contact because we've been recommended, which is fantastic. But, if you don't know anyone who can recommend a great bookkeeper, where do you start and what should you look for?

▶ **Look at bookkeeping directories**

The first place to look is the websites of the main bookkeeping and accounting organisations. I'd suggest viewing the directory of the Institute for Certified Bookkeepers (ICB); this has a search function which allows you to find a local bookkeeper using your postcode and the services you're looking for.

▶ **Check the bookkeeper's website**

Once you've found a bookkeeper you think might be able to help, take a look at their website to find out more about them.

You'll want to find out:

» The services they provide (and costs, if available)

» The type of clients they work with, whether their clients are in the same industry or face similar challenges to you

» Information about the bookkeeper's qualifications and experience

▶ **Review their LinkedIn profile**

LinkedIn is a great way to find out about the bookkeeper's work experience and qualifications, and there might be some testimonials from previous clients which will help you learn more about their work.

▶ **See what they're doing on social media**

Although this one isn't as important for understanding the quality of the bookkeeper's work, it's a good idea to check whether the bookkeeper is a good fit for your business and the industry you work in. One way of doing that is by looking at the conversations they're having on social media and the content they're posting. You want to know that your bookkeeper understands your industry, and this can be a good place to start.

> ▶ **Have an initial chat**

Once you feel like you've got an idea of the bookkeeper's background, give them a call and talk to them about your business, the type of the support you need, and their experience, particularly whether they've worked with similar clients in the past. Speaking to them will really help you gauge whether or not they're a good fit for you and your business. People often get in touch with us by email or through the contact form on the website requesting that we set up a meeting. I almost always start with a quick chat on the phone as it gives us both the opportunity to see whether we're a good fit.

Why you shouldn't employ the cheapest bookkeeper

A few years ago, I had a new kitchen fitted and, as somebody who doesn't know anything about building or fitting kitchens, I asked three builders to quote for the work. The first turned up with his dad and quoted me a price which was half of my budget. The second turned up in his very nice-looking van and quoted me three times the price of the first. The third turned up, gave me some suggestions of ways I could improve the layout, add more light and get the best deal on my tiles, and quoted me a price somewhere in-between. In true Goldilocks-style, I went with him.

When you're starting any project, be it a kitchen or getting your finances in order, you need to have the best people on hand to help you. Of course, price is a factor but hiring the cheapest supplier doesn't always pay.

> ▶ **They might not have the right qualifications**

Anyone can call themselves a bookkeeper or even an accountant; whether they have the right qualifications to do so, however, is another matter. It can take years to complete professional training. To obtain a practice licence from the Institute of Certified Bookkeepers (ICB), a bookkeeper needs to take up to 7 exams. There are additional exams if you want to offer extra services such as preparing tax returns or payroll. As an accountant I can also tell you that I took 14 exams over four years alongside my full-time job to achieve my accountancy qualification. Bookkeepers and accountants who are members of professional bodies are also obliged to complete and document CPD (Continuing Professional Development) to refresh their knowledge and skills each year. To be sure you're working with somebody who really knows what they're doing, you need to quiz them on their credentials.

A qualified bookkeeper will know the value of their time and will charge a rate which is reflective of the knowledge and skill they can bring to your business. Somebody who is not qualified might place a lower value on their time, being more likely to charge a rate closer to the minimum wage, and risks come with hiring those people.

▶ They might be inexperienced

I recently saw a post in a bookkeepers' Facebook group where somebody had applied for a bookkeeping job but didn't know how to use Excel or the accounting system mentioned in the advert. I discourage my clients from using Excel, but it is still a key piece of software used in the industry, and I was surprised that somebody applying for this kind of role was unable to use it. It made me question their work experience. If somebody is quoting a very low rate for bookkeeping work, it might be because they lack experience and don't have the confidence to charge more.

▶ They might not have the right paperwork

As bookkeepers, we are obliged to have the right paperwork in place. But the Books, for example, has a practice licence from the ICB, professional insurance, we're registered with the Information Commissioner's Office for purposes of data protection and GDPR (the General Data Protection

Regulation), and we check out all of our clients so that we meet the requirements of Money Laundering Regulations. A cheap bookkeeper might not have the right licences and documentation and you should always check before hiring a bookkeeper to ensure that they're properly qualified and insured.

> ► **They might be putting your data at risk**

Sometimes bookkeepers are particularly cheap because they outsource work to people outside the UK. I have no issue with subcontracting—I sometimes subcontract work myself—but if your work is outsourced to a country which doesn't observe the requirements of GDPR, your data could be at risk. Additionally, if your data is outsourced to somebody who doesn't understand UK accounting regulations, this could result in errors in your accounts, resulting in you potentially submitting incorrect information to HMRC or Companies House or you paying an accountant or bookkeeper a hefty sum to correct your accounts.

> ► **It might cost you more in the long run**

Let's say you hire a bookkeeper who is charging £10 per hour. They take longer to do your bookkeeping because they're inexperienced or they need to rework it because they've made errors. Even worse, you might even have to hire somebody else to smooth out the errors they've made. This is going to cost you a lot more than the £10 per hour you originally expected to pay. When comparing quotes, make sure you factor in skill and experience when reviewing the price.

Fee expectations

I've given a number of reasons why you should avoid employing the cheapest bookkeeper, but how much should you expect to pay?

Traditionally, bookkeepers charged an hourly rate and I've seen this range from the minimum wage to £40 per hour depending on qualifications and experience. I know accountants from accounting firms who charge significantly more per hour. More and more, though, I'm meeting bookkeepers who charge a fixed fee which is linked to the value they add to your business rather than an hourly rate. This is almost always how we work at But the Books. We've found that our customers want to know what they're going to pay up front rather than having to wait until we've completed the task. Simply think of it the way you'd think of employing somebody on a salary rather than on an hourly rate contract.

When you're making your decision about who to work with, fees will play a part. In order to judge whether those fees are justified, as well as finding out how long it will take to complete your work, read up on their skills, training and work experience, as the bookkeeper's fee should reflect all of these things. Also, and most importantly, consider the value they will add to your business. This can be quite difficult to measure, but you can't put a price on peace of mind.

Another way to judge whether the cost of outsourcing something like bookkeeping is worth paying is to consider how much your own time is worth. If your bookkeeper gives you back two days per month, what could you be earning with those two days rather than losing them to bookkeeping? Even if you're just outsourcing your tax return, how long does it usually take you to do and what could you be doing with that time instead?

Once you know that, the decision to outsource should be an easy one.

How to prepare for your first meeting with your bookkeeper

Once you've chosen a bookkeeper or at least whittled the choice down to one or two, you'll want to make sure that you get the most from your initial meeting. Here are some things to think about before you go.

✓ **Be clear on what you want your bookkeeper to do for you**

You probably spoke to them about this in your initial chat, but it's important for both you and them to be absolutely clear on what you need. You might want them to look after your full monthly process. You might prefer to keep a lot of it in-house, simply asking them to run specific processes. Like Lisa, you might just want them to take on a one-off project for you.

✓ Get your paperwork ready

Believe me, bookkeepers have seen it all! The main thing is to get everything together that your bookkeeper might need to understand your business finances.

This includes:

» Your bank statements

» Invoices you've raised to customers

» Expense receipts received

» Invoices received from suppliers

» A list of all your sources of income, whether transfers are made to your bank account post-invoice, via paypal or some other payment method

Your bookkeeper will also need access to the spreadsheet you're keeping for your business finances or your accounting system if you have one, and to know when you last updated it.

✓ List your questions

Make a list of any questions you have or anything you're not sure of, any specific requests you have for your bookkeeper—such as if you want your sales to be divided into specific categories—and any problems you've experienced when recording transactions. This list will guide the conversation in your meeting and ensure that your bookkeeper is aware of any challenges that you're facing. It will also give them the opportunity to warn you if they don't offer a service that you require.

✓ Answer your bookkeeper's requests for information

Your bookkeeper probably sent you a questionnaire following your initial call. They need to understand certain things about your business and will have a list of questions to help them. They also need to make sure that they can verify your identity, so they will have asked you for certain pieces of information and to provide ID, so make sure you have this available at your meeting.

✓ Think about software

Your bookkeeper will talk to you about your accounting records and will want to address the question of software if you're not already using some. Find out which software they favour and do some research online and ask any other business owners you know; this will help you gauge your preferences before you meet. Most of the main software providers offer a free trial, so you might find it worthwhile to sign up and have a play around before your meeting.

Summary

In this chapter we've talked about what a bookkeeper does and how they can help your business, both in terms of the tasks they can complete but also the value they can add to your business through their skills and experience and the peace of mind they'll give you.

We've looked at how to find a good bookkeeper, how to assess whether they're right for you and your business, and how choosing the cheapest may well be a false economy. Actually, I can't stress this point enough. If you're going to outsource your bookkeeping, find a great bookkeeper or firm with the right qualifications and brilliant testimonials written by clients just like you. You'll find that they're the best investment you've ever made. It's easy to find a great bookkeeper by checking directories, where you can find qualified bookkeeping professionals in your area and see at a glance which skills and specialisms they can offer.

Once you've found a bookkeeper, prepare well so that you can make the most of your initial meeting and ensure that you get off to a great start. You'll never look back.

AFTERWORD

You made it! So, tell me something. Which one word sums up how you feel when you think about bookkeeping?

When I posted an Instagram story asking people which one word came to mind when they thought of bookkeeping, people said 'scary', 'taxing', 'shudder', 'fiddly' and simply 'urghhhh'. Perhaps one of those words resonated with you before you started reading this book. How do you feel now?

Over the last 11 chapters, we've looked at your motivation for doing your bookkeeping, who's going to do it and when. We've looked at why people struggle with money and numbers and how to tackle your numbers in a logical, emotion-free way.

We then moved on to look at the kinds of questions I'm asked all the time by small businesses, either when they're just starting up or when they're a few years in to trading. We've looked at legal structures, how different types of businesses are taxed, how you can pay yourself and, really importantly, why you should have a separate bank account for your business if you don't already.

We've looked at how to deal with your backlog of paperwork (probably one of the things which overwhelms our clients the most), accounting systems, and then implementing a regular process which you can follow and maintain.

I've told you a bit about accountancy and the mistakes people often make with their bookkeeping. We've looked at the main business reports, budgeting and forecasting and then KPIs and how you can use them to really understand your business.

Hopefully you now feel much more confident in your ability to keep good records for your business or at least you know where to start, but I know that bookkeeping isn't for everyone. Often when we start businesses, we have to do everything for the business because we have insufficient funds to outsource things. There might come a time, though, when you decide to outsource, whether this is to give you some time back or because you need a bookkeeper's expertise. So, I finished off by talking about how to find a good bookkeeper and how to get the most out of working with them.

My parting advice to you is to do what you love, do what you are best at, and if bookkeeping isn't that thing then there's no shame in outsourcing it. There are people like me and the team at But the Books who genuinely do love doing this stuff.

I hope that you've taken away some great lessons from this book, that you feel more confident with your business finances and that you're ready to start tracking some KPIs to really help you *know your numbers*. And of course, if you want to speak to some great bookkeepers, we're always here to help and we'd love to hear from you.

www.butthebooks.co.uk

GLOSSARY

Accountant

An accountant is a person who reports on the financial performance of a business. Accountants work with the financial data provided to them, building upon the work done by bookkeepers to produce financial statements and reports.

Small businesses hire accountants to support them at the end of the year with filing limited company accounts to Companies House and corporation tax returns to HMRC.

Accountants should be properly qualified with an accounting body; some of the best well known are the Association of Chartered Certified Accountants (ACCA), the Chartered Institute of Management Accountants (CIMA) and the Institute of Certified Accountants in England and Wales (ICAEW).

Accounts payable

This is the money your business owes to its suppliers. Accounts payable are sometimes known as trade creditors.

Accounts receivable

This is the money that is owed to your business by your customers. Accounts receivable are sometimes known as trade debtors.

Accrual

A cost that relates to the current period but for which you haven't yet received the invoice. Adjustments for accruals are usually made as part of the year end processes for businesses accounting under the accruals concept. Accruals are not relevant for sole traders using the cash basis.

Accruals basis

Most businesses do their accounting using the accruals basis. This is the traditional way of accounting. It means that transactions are recorded in the business's accounts based on the date the transaction took place rather than the date cash moved in or out of the bank account. It's important for giving an accurate picture of the true income and costs of a business over a financial period. Limited companies must report using the accruals concept; sole traders with a small turnover may use the cash basis if they prefer.

Actuals

Your *actual* financial figures, what really happened. Actuals can be compared to budgets to calculate variances.

Aged payables report

A report which shows balances due to suppliers. It's usually set out as a table with a list of suppliers down the side with periods along the top indicating the amount due to each supplier and the time frame it's due within.

Aged receivables report

A report which shows balances due from customers. Similar to the aged payables report, it's set out as a table with a list of customers down the side with periods along the top. It will indicate amounts which are not yet due, usually listed as 'current', and then amounts which are 0-30 days overdue, 30-60 days overdue, 60-90 days overdue and then amounts 90+ days overdue.

Asset

An asset is an item owned by the business for use within the business (such as a machine), or something which can be easily turned into cash (such as stock or accounts receivable). Assets appear on the Balance Sheet of a business.

Balance Sheet

A business's Balance Sheet is a financial statement which shows what the business owes, what it owns, and how it has been funded at a set point in time. A Balance Sheet is called this because it's driven by a formula which needs to *balance:*

$$\textbf{Equity} = \text{Assets} - \text{Liabilities}$$

If the values don't balance, then a mistake has been made somewhere in the accounts. The Balance Sheet can be used to calculate a number of KPIs to measure how a business's financial health is changing over time.

Bookkeeper

A bookkeeper is a person employed to record a business's financial transactions in the business's accounting system. The bookkeeper will usually be responsible for recording the sales, purchases, and payroll. They will make sure transactions from the bank account are properly recorded and can submit VAT returns where required. A bookkeeper should have a qualification from a bookkeeping body, such as the Institute of Certified Bookkeepers, but will not usually be an accountant.

Budget

A budget sets out how much income and expenditure you expect your business to earn in the coming months and years and therefore how much profit will be made. A budget is usually built for the 12 months ahead but could be built for any period. You can track your actual performance against your budget each month to see where you're over or underspending so you can change course if necessary.

Cash basis

Sole traders below the VAT threshold are able to keep their accounting records using the cash basis if they wish to. This means that transactions are recorded at the date the cash goes through the bank account, rather than using invoice dates. This makes bookkeeping more straightforward for very small businesses, but it's not applicable to larger sole traders or limited companies as they must use the accruals basis.

Cash flow forecast

A cash flow forecast is a useful way of seeing how much money you'll have in the bank at a point in the future. It can be built using a spreadsheet or specialist software and relies upon an existing estimation of what your income and expenditure will be in coming months. This information can be taken from your budget if you have one.

Cost of sales

This is the cost of expenditure directly linked to producing the goods or services that you sell. It includes costs of the product(s) you sell, manufacturing costs, and costs of hiring people to deliver your services. It does not include overheads.

Creditor

A creditor is somebody to whom you owe money. It includes trade creditors—your suppliers—and others you owe money to such as the bank if you have a loan or overdraft, and potentially HMRC if you owe taxes.

Current assets

These are assets of the business which will change in value or be used up within the space of a year. Current assets include cash, accounts receivable and stock. You'll see the term 'Current Assets' on your Balance Sheet.

Current liabilities

These are liabilities which will change in value or be paid off within the next year. Current liabilities include accounts payable and short-term debts such as overdrafts.

Debtor

A debtor is somebody who owes you money. This includes accounts receivable or customers but could also include HMRC if, for example, you'd made an overpayment.

Debtor days

The average number of days it takes your customers to pay you.

Debtor days = Debtors / Average Daily Sales.

Director's loan

When a director takes money out of their limited company without putting it through payroll and when it hasn't been declared as a dividend, this money is a loan from the business to the director and is categorised as director's loan.

Dividend

This is a distribution of a limited company's profits to its shareholders.

Drawings

When a sole trader takes money out of their business, this is classed as drawings. It is not a salary and therefore not an expense of the business, as a sole trader and their business are the same legal entity and so the business's money belongs to them. The opposite of drawings is capital or funds introduced.

Equity

Equity is the value of the owners' investment in a business, or the difference between a business's assets and liabilities.

Financial Year

This is the year for which a business reports its activity. Limited companies' financial years are determined by when the company was first registered, although the year end date can be changed if necessary. Companies prepare their financial reports and tax returns for the business's financial year. Sole traders may also choose to work to financial year dates of their choosing, but are bound to the dates of the UK's tax year which runs from April 6th until April 5th.

Fixed assets

These are assets—things the business owns—which will be held in the business for a long time. Fixed assets include property, machinery and other equipment. Fixed assets appear on the Balance Sheet.

Gross profit

Gross profit is the profit made on your sales once you have deducted the costs directly involved in making those products or services available for sale. If you don't make a very high gross profit or you make a loss, you will struggle to cover your overheads or make a net profit.

$$\textbf{Gross Profit} = \text{Sales} - \text{Cost of Sales}$$

Gross profit margin

Gross profit margin is gross profit expressed as a percentage of sales. You can monitor your gross profit margin against a budgeted figure, against previous periods or against the gross profit margin of other products or services you sell.

$$\textbf{Gross Profit Margin} = \text{Gross Profit} / \text{Sales x } 100\%$$

Income statement

This is another term for the Profit and Loss report.

Inventory

This is another term for stock.

Key Performance Indicator (KPI)

This is a measure you can calculate and track to understand something about your business.

Liability

A liability is a debt, person or bill which you need to repay. Liabilities appear on the Balance Sheet.

Liquidity

Liquidity refers to the health of your cash flow.

Making Tax Digital

Making Tax Digital (MTD) aims to reduce errors in tax returns filed to HMRC. HMRC want to move individuals and businesses from keeping manual records on paper and spreadsheets to software.

Net profit

This is the profit made after deducting all the expenses incurred.

Net Profit = Sales - Cost of Sales - Overheads

Net profit margin

This is net profit expressed as a percentage of sales.

Net Profit Margin = Net Profit / Sales x 100%

Open banking

Open banking refers to financial technology which allows software to have access to bank account information.

Overheads

These are the costs of running the business which are not directly related to the product or service you sell. Generally, you need to pay them just to keep the business running and they include costs of rent, power, marketing and your website as well as other administrative costs and costs of management staff.

Prepayment

This is where you pay for a product or service in the period before you consume it. You need to identify and account for any prepayments if you use the accruals basis for accounting.

Profit & Loss (P&L) report

This report shows you the business's income, expenditure and profit. It can be run for any period to compare sales, costs and profits from month to month and year to year.

Revenue

Another word for sales or turnover.

Self-assessment tax return

This is a declaration made to HMRC every year for anybody with untaxed income such as sole traders. A return is completed and the amount of tax due to HMRC is calculated.

Share capital

When a limited company is set up, a number of shares are usually sold to shareholders in exchange for cash, which becomes the equity of the business. Shares appear on the Balance Sheet.

Stock

This is any asset which is held for the purpose of being sold on to customers to make a profit. Stock in hand will show on the Balance Sheet.

Trade payables

This is the specific group of creditors or payables whom the business owes money in respect of purchases of goods or stock which would come under the heading of 'Cost of Sales'. Other payables for administrative costs and taxes would not fall under this heading.

Trade receivables

This is the specific group of debtors or receivables who owe the business money in respect of purchases made from the business.

Turnover

This is another word for sales or revenue.

Variance

In the context of budgeting, this is the difference between budgeted and actual figures. A favourable variance occurs when more income is generated than budgeted, or costs are lower than budgeted. An adverse variance occurs when less income is generated than budgeted, or costs are more than budgeted.

Year-end accounts

These for a report which sets out a business's financial performance at the end of its accounting year. Limited companies are required to prepare and file year-end accounts with Companies House.

MONTHLY FINANCE CHECKLIST

Customers

- ☐ Send invoices to each of your customers for work completed in the month

- ☐ Bank cash and cheques received from customers

- ☐ Run an aged receivables report to check your customers have paid you

- ☐ Chase late payments

Suppliers

- ☐ Record supplier invoices received in your accounting system

- ☐ Run an aged payables report to identify invoices due for payment

- ☐ Pay outstanding supplier invoices

Expenses

- ☐ Record business expenses in your accounting system

- ☐ Upload expense receipts to your accounting system or file them

Banking

- ☐ Record all transactions from the bank statement in your accounting system

- ☐ Find paperwork for transactions without an invoice or expense receipt

- ☐ Reconcile the month-end balance on your bank statement against your accounting system

Payroll (if you're an employer)

- ☐ Run payroll

- ☐ Issue payslips and any relevant documents to employees

- ☐ Submit relevant returns to HMRC

- ☐ Pay PAYE, NI, student loan deductions to HMRC

- ☐ Pay pension deductions to pension provider

VAT (if you're VAT registered)

- ☐ Review your VAT position

- ☐ Complete your VAT return if due

- ☐ Pay VAT liability to HMRC

Links and resources

1. But the Books - www.butthebooks.co.uk

2. HMRC's guide to setting up as a sole trader www.gov.uk/set-up-sole-trader

3. HMRC's guide to setting up a limited company www.gov.uk/set-up-limited-company

ABOUT THE AUTHOR

Zoe Whitman is the founder of But the Books, a bookkeeping practice in Bristol which helps small business owners who know how to do everything in business... but the books. But the Books won the ICB's Small Practice of the Year award in 2018 after less than two years in business. In 2019 they were shortlisted as one of the finalists for the British Accountancy Awards' Independent Firm of the Year – South West, and Zoe was named one of Enterprise Nation's Top 50 Advisers.

But the Books was set up as Zoe's side hustle in 2017, and she ran the business part-time alongside her job as an accountant until the time she decided to take the business full-time in 2018. But the Books now has a team of four and is growing every day.

Zoe qualified as an accountant in 2006; she has a degree in Applied Accounting, and she's worked for the likes of BT, the BBC and Lloyds Banking Group after spending the start of her career in local government. She is a qualified bookkeeper, and But the Books holds a bookkeeping licence from the Institute of Certified Bookkeepers.

Zoe is regularly quoted in industry press, including AAT Comment, Accountancy Age, and the ACCA's Accounting and Business Magazine. She writes articles for the Institute of Certified Bookkeepers and is a columnist for AccountingWEB. She's also a regular on the AccountingWEB podcast.

With 16 years' industry experience and having run her own bookkeeping practice since 2017, it's more than likely Zoe's worked with a business just like yours. In fact, she's embarked on a journey just like yours, too. If you want to feel in control of your finances, Zoe's the one to help.

You can follow them on Twitter and/or Instagram @but_the_books. Or you can contact Zoe and the But the Books team through their website www.butthebooks.co.uk

ACKNOWLEDGEMENTS

I didn't plan to be an accountant. In fact, there was a time when my life ambition was to be a supervisor in a national chemist chain: there's not a huge amount of ambition in seaside towns. Fast forward a few years and I find myself on my first day as a trainee accountant in local government. My boss had offered to pay for my accountancy training and the way I understood it, my job would be to make spreadsheets and to do lots of photocopying. I didn't know how to use a spreadsheet but I did know how to use a photocopier, so I took the job.

My boss used to call me into meetings with anyone and everyone. He'd ask me to make cups of tea and then get me to stay for the rest of the meeting. I didn't realise it then, but those meetings built my people skills and taught me about the business I worked in, the services I was accounting for, the budgets I was helping to monitor and the challenges the service managers—my clients—were facing.

As I got older I got tired of working for other people. I found myself listening to entrepreneurship podcasts, being positively brainwashed by productivity books and longing for the opportunity to put it all into practice in my own business. But there was something important to me about security of income every month. There was something about the uncertainty of starting my own business which put it completely out of reach.

I did some voluntary work, helping young people who were starting their businesses with their accounts and then one day I got talking to a barista in a coffee shop who wanted to be a violin teacher but was afraid of becoming self-employed because he'd have to do a tax return, and that was the spark of the idea.

Having my daughter and being given the gift of a whole year off work meant I was able to finally start something, a business which seemed to grow exponentially on the goodwill of Bristol's vibrant creative sector. I told myself it was a side hustle, but I knew it was what I was supposed to be doing with my life. After six months back in my "real job", one Sunday sat on a hill in the sunshine while my daughter had a nap and I took a call from a client I simply didn't have time to speak to on any other day of the week, we decided as a family that I should leave my job to take the business full-time. I resigned the next day. It's the scariest thing I've ever done.

A year on, I employ a lovely team of people and I'm juggling the business alongside my daughter who is now a busy toddler, and my son who has kept me awake enough to write much of this book on my phone in the dark during night feeds. I'm still scared every day but I'm also excited. I make a difference to people, and I know it because people hug me in meetings. I love what we do at But the Books and I love the new challenges that each day brings. This book wouldn't have been possible without my children giving me the opportunity to focus on what really matters to me, my husband who pushed me to make it happen, or the small businesses who took a risk and employed a start-up to look after their books.

I especially want to acknowledge and thank the ICB who have supported me on this journey and to Garry for writing the foreword to this book.

Thank you to the clients (off the top of my head James, Joel, Gareth, Damian, Tom, Debs, Gaby, Lesley, Emmeline and Zoe but I know there are so many more) who didn't blink an eye when I've turned up to meetings with a baby, nor did they once question my ability to perform and deliver what they needed for their businesses even when I was heavily pregnant or breastfeeding a newborn on a video call.

I must thank Carla and Rose, my first employees who've looked after the business as if it was their own, and Faye and the Freelance Mum community for the warmth and incredible support you've all shown me. Running a business isn't for the faint-hearted and I'm so grateful to have you all at my side.

In terms of making the book happen, thank you to Alexa from The Book Refinery who told me I had to write these acknowledgements, and who held my hand through the publishing process, and to Katrina who didn't come and work for me as an intern but who through that wonderful way the world works became my proofreader instead. Thank you also to Delia and Geoff who often bring me food and who read the whole book cover to cover, kindly updating me on how boring it was every time they saw me during the proofreading phase.

I must thank Friska, Cook and Deliveroo who make up for my inability to put a meal together most days, and on a completely unrelated note Mr Bell who taught me what a rectangular hyperbola is, and who played a large part in helping me realise that I might have a future beyond that job in the chemist.

I want to thank Abi who reminded me about happiness and Nikki who I can always talk through my ideas with.

And finally I want to thank Olly, Heidi and Wilf, because you are everything.

Printed in Great Britain
by Amazon

45736144R00093